EASY
EXOTIC

EASY EXOTIC

A Model's Low-Fat Recipes
from Around the World

PADMA LAKSHMI
WITH GEORGIA DOWNARD

FOOD PHOTOGRAPHY BY
ELIZABETH WATT

MIRAMAX
B O O K S
HYPERION
NEW YORK

Copyright © 1999 by Padma Lakshmi

Food photography by Elizabeth Watt.
Cover photo by Priscilla Benedetti.
Photos of Padma pp. vi, 27, 31, 58, 113, by Priscilla Benedetti.

Library of Congress Cataloging-In-Publication Data

Lakshmi, Padma.
    Easy exotic : a model's low-fat recipes from around the world / Padma
Lakshmi with Georgia Downard.—1st. ed.
        p.   cm.
    1. Entrées (Cookery)   2. Cookery, International.   3. Quick and
easy cookery.   4. Low-fat diet—Recipes.   I. Downard, Georgia.
II. Title.
TX740.L289   1999
641.8'2—dc21   98-26336
                                                        CIP

ISBN 0-7868-6459-1

First Edition

10 9 8 7 6 5 4 3 2 1

This book is dedicated to Amma,
K.C.K., T.K.A., and Old Spingler

Acknowledgments

The author wishes to thank Paula Bonelli; Priscilla Benedetti; Mrs. Gabrielle Castiglione; Louis Claudio; Susan Dalsimer; Georgia Downard; Ricardo Gay; Andrea Griminelli; Renate Horvath; Arturo & Maria of Latteria San Marco, Milan, Italy; Mirella Liberait; Marco Maachi Renato and his parents of Ristorante Rigolo, Milan, Italy; Virginia Moore; Shayna Pelavin; Piero Piazi; Kristin Powers; Peter Prasad; Rick Schwartz; Tina Sharpe; Lisa Sacco; Elizabeth Watt; and Harvey Weinstein.

Contents

Preface

A good cook is like a sorceress who dispenses happiness.
—Elsa Schiaparelli

Throughout my adolescence in the States I had been approached by different people who thought I should model. My mother's ideas on the subject were quite clear. If I was beautiful at seventeen, I would be beautiful at twenty-one when I graduated from college. She was, as always, right. My last semester of college I went to study in Spain. While hanging out in a Madrid pub one fateful night I was discovered and sent on my first modeling job.

Since then I have finished a bachelor's degree in theater arts, lived in Milan, Paris, and New York, and learned much about myself and the world at large. My first taste of walking down a runway was intimidating to say the least. I had been booked to do a Ralph Lauren show in New York, and for my first entrance was flanked by Stephanie Seymour and Christy Turlington. Since then I have walked for such designers as Isaac Mizrahi, Sonia Rykiel, Romeo Gigli, Giorgio Armani, Valentino, Herve Leger, and Moschino. I have worked with photographers such as Helmut Newton, Aldo Fallai, and Fabrizio Ferri.

Traveling from city to city during collections has quite a grueling effect on body and spirit. It was during these times that I began to rediscover my skills as a chef. Making recipes from my childhood made me feel less homesick, and controlling my diet through healthier versions of classic recipes kept my waistline in check.

Modeling in different fashion shoots in exotic places also contributed to my culinary repertoire. My first big editorial shoot was in Morocco for Italian *Elle* where I learned about fiery Harissa and couscous. While shooting French lingerie in Bali, I learned how to make a low-calorie fish (Bali baked fish) I tasted there.

After each of my trips I always brought back some exotic herb or spice to enhance my recipes: tamarind from Mexico, sun-dried tomatoes from San Remo. In fact, fusing different cultures into one dish became a great adventure in my kitchen; you will find a recipe for raita (an Indian dish) attached to the Moroccan upma (which is really an Indian dish made with couscous). Indeed, the best part of modeling for me was traveling and increasing my knowledge of world cultures.

I finished my first film this past summer in Cuba. The irony was that the director wanted me to gain weight for my character, a Native American warrior from the 1600s. Gaining weight in Cuba proved quite easy with a steady diet of pork chops and fried plantains. Yet when I came back to the States, I quickly remembered that what was good for my role in the movie was not at all what was required from a fashion model. I had to promptly lose those extra pounds, yet I knew that dieting in the traditional sense was a foreign concept to me. So I relied on my own culinary skills. Cutting out fried foods, butter, cream, and excessive amounts of red meat, I updated all these international recipes I had gathered through the years. Mixing them for variety, I soon had a collection of dishes as diverse as the places I had been. Word got out among my friends who were also concerned with eating healthy and I found myself handing out recipes to them as well.

Food influences and inspires me as much as my profession as a model does; it permeates my life in the same way the aroma of a spicy curry can linger in a home for days. Cooking has enabled me to provide for others in a very real way. Never underestimate the power of a good bowl of warm food. Indeed, at times when my professional life got unbearable, my spirit saved the day.

Cooking has always been as much a demonstration of my self-worth as my modeling paychecks have been, and at times, it has been an even more tangible proof of my value. I may not work for a while, but I can always demonstrate my usefulness in the kitchen. A memory of something my grandfather said once while looking at pictures of potential matrimonial matches for my uncle still haunts me, "Yes, she is very pretty, but can she make a decent bowl of rice?"

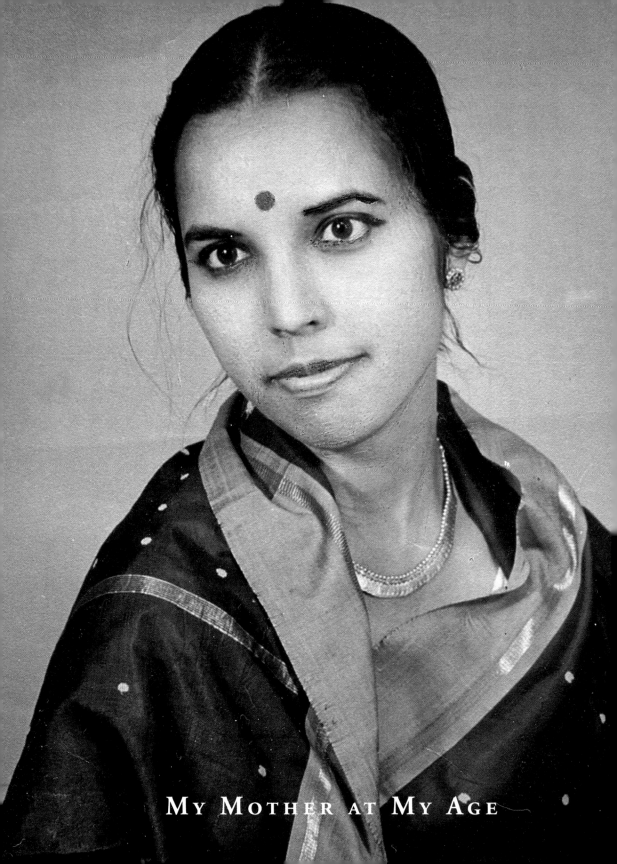

MY MOTHER AT MY AGE

All the women in my family knew how to create magic in the kitchen. Not only for whom they cooked, but for those of us who were around while they were creating it. Some of the warmest memories I have of growing up in South India originate in the kitchen, memories that would later lay the foundation for my love of cooking. During my childhood I remember the women chattering as we sat on the cool marble floor shelling peas, grating coconut, or stealing every third piece of sour mango from my aunt's rations for chutney. The women seemed so completely possessed by the spirit of what they were doing.

Soon the men would trickle into the kitchen, the women would disperse, and I would cling to my grandmother's sari as she lit the evening prayer lamps, which were kept in the pantry connected to the kitchen. It is no accident that in Madras and other south Indian towns and cities the prayer—or puja—room is often near the kitchen. The offering of special foods in various religious ceremonies always played the biggest role in bringing the family together. From the simple stringing together of lemon garlands for the goddess Durga, to dividing the *prasadam* or blessed foods for the children first, I came to associate food not only with femininity, but also with purity, and divinity. There was always a respect given to food, a dignity demonstrated in its preparation, and an honor to serving a well-received meal.

Since those days on the floor of my grandmother's kitchen, my life has changed quite a bit. I have learned other recipes from my various travels. Unlike most Westerners I have gone from being a vegetarian (I was brought up in the strictest of Brahmin households) to eating meat. Perhaps the biggest change for me has been taking shortcuts in the kitchen. I am no longer able to spend hours picking over peas or grating coconut. Every time I open a can or bottle, I long for the luxury of having everything made from scratch with the goodness that can only come from the freshest of ingredients. But now, if I allowed myself to be discouraged by using a bouillon cube instead of making my own stock, I'd probably never step in the kitchen again. Because of my job, I have also resorted to using fat-free mayonnaise and low-fat foods whenever feasible. This is not in any way diet food. No one ever sticks to diets, because they often take away the pleasure of flavor. I suppose this could be called "happy medium" food. It is prepared relatively fast, and it is not gravely fattening because it avoids things like cream and butter. What I will not do is eat food that does not taste good.

> Most people love to eat. There's a real celebratory aspect to a great meal—a sensuality and a theatricality to it.
>
> —*Stanley Tucci*

My last semester at Clark University I became stir-crazy, itching to sample another culture. Although I had never taken a Spanish class in my life, I convinced the foreign languages department to send me to Spain to study. Indeed my Spanish vocabulary consisted mostly of culinary terms.

It was in Madrid where I first started to model. I ate in humble eating establishments rather than trendy restaurants and developed a taste for five o'clock *tapas.* Because I was raised in an old British colony, *tapas* appealed to my love of *tiffin* (similar to afternoon tea), and I must say I came to prefer a small glass of beer to the cup of tea I usually had.

S
P
A
I
N

SPANISH STUFFED BELL PEPPERS

BELL PEPPERS FILLED WITH CURRIED RICE AND VEAL

There was a small café called the Bahia near the Tandem Institute where I went to school that had an impressive menu of beautiful and delicious dishes. The one I've included lends itself to being a light meal, but I have substituted ground veal for the usual beef and added some ginger.

Prep Time: *20 to 25 minutes*
Cook Time: *40 to 45 minutes*

6 green, red, or yellow bell peppers, or a combination

1 tablespoon olive oil, plus additional for drizzling tops of peppers

1 onion, minced

2 large garlic cloves, minced, or to taste

1 teaspoon hot Madras curry powder, or to taste*

1 teaspoon ground ginger

3 cups cooked long-grain rice, preferably Basmati

1 pound ground veal

10 ounce package frozen peas, cooked according to package directions

3 firm, ripe tomatoes, diced

1 tablespoon minced fresh oregano, or 1 teaspoon dried oregano, crumbled

3 tablespoons minced fresh cilantro, or to taste

Salt to taste

Cayenne pepper to taste (optional)

3 tablespoons fresh or dry bread crumbs

Lemon juice or wedges

1. Preheat oven to 375°F.

2. Cut off tops of peppers and remove seeds and ribs, reserving tops. Discard stems and dice reserved tops. Set aside.

3. In a large saucepan of boiling water blanch the peppers for 3 to 4 min-

*Available at specialty food shops

utes, or until they are slightly soft. Drain, refresh, and pat dry. Cut off a thin slice from the bottom of each pepper so that it stands straight.

4. In a nonstick skillet set over moderate heat, warm 1 tablespoon olive oil until it is hot, add the onion and reserved diced pepper and cook, stirring occasionally, for 3 to 5 minutes, or until vegetables are softened. Add the garlic, curry powder, and ginger, and cook, stirring, 2 minutes. Transfer mixture to a large bowl.

5. Add the remaining ingredients, except the bread crumbs and lemon, to the bowl and gently stir to combine well.

6. Stuff the peppers with the filling and arrange them in a shallow baking pan. Sprinkle tops of peppers with the bread crumbs and drizzle each with a little olive oil.

7. Bake the peppers for 40 to 45 minutes, or until stuffing is completely cooked. Transfer peppers to a serving platter and sprinkle with lemon juice or serve with lemon wedges.

Serves 6.

(Per serving) Calories: 557; Protein: 25g; Fat: 8g;
Carbohydrates: 95g; Cholesterol: 62mg; Sodium: 164mg.

Cookery is not chemistry. It is an art. It requires instinct and taste rather than exact measurements.

—*X. Marcel Boulestin*

SPANISH TORTILLA CAKE

POTATO, ONION, AND EGG OMELETTE

Between hunting down addresses for castings in every corner of Madrid and mornings full of intensive Spanish lessons, often I didn't have time for a full lunch so I would go to the nearest bar for a cup of hot café con leche and a warm slice of Tortilla Cake.

Prep Time: *10 minutes*
Cook Time: *25 minutes*

3 tablespoons olive oil

1 large onion, thinly sliced

1 tablespoon minced fresh rosemary
 leaves, or 1 teaspoon dried rosemary,
 crumbled

1½ teaspoons minced fresh thyme
 leaves, or ½ teaspoon dried thyme,
 crumbled

Salt and freshly ground black pepper
 to taste

6 large eggs

4 egg whites

2 pounds (about 3 large) potatoes,
 boiled, peeled, and sliced

1. In a large nonstick skillet set over moderate heat, warm 1 tablespoon of the oil until it is hot, add the onion, rosemary, thyme, salt, and pepper and cook, stirring occasionally, for 5 to 7 minutes, or until onion is golden. Let cool.

2. In a bowl whisk together the whole eggs, egg whites, and some salt and pepper to taste. Add the onions and stir to combine.

3. In the skillet heat 1 tablespoon oil until hot over moderate heat, add the egg mixture and cook just until edges begin to set, about 3 minutes. Add the potatoes, spreading them in an even layer, reduce the heat to moderately low, and cook, covered, for 6 to 8 minutes, or until eggs are almost completely set. Place a plate over the omelette and invert the omelette onto the plate. Set skillet back on heat, add remaining oil, turning pan to coat bottom with oil, and slip omelette back into pan. Cook for 3 minutes more, or until bottom is just set.

4. Transfer omelette to serving dish. Cut into wedges and serve hot or warm.

Serves 6.

(Per serving) Calories: 236; Protein: 10g; Fat: 11g;
Carbohydrates: 23g; Cholesterol: 181mg; Sodium: 143mg.

I did my first photo shoot outside of Toledo. We had started early in the morning and by eleven I was already hungry enough for a hearty lunch. The Spanish prairie is stunning at any time of the year, but it was a cold February morning, and there was no place to eat for miles. With my summer hat blowing in the winter wind, I pleaded with the photographer for lunch. He told me he hadn't planned on stopping for lunch: the next shot would be me in a pair of tight shorts and he didn't want my stomach bulging.

We finally took a break. I went into the location van and the stylist produced a small carafe of red wine from her bag. "This will warm you up," she said. She handed me a Styrofoam cup and produced two sandwiches wrapped in aluminum foil. I gratefully took one. I had never eaten seafood until then, but hunger had torn a hole in my stomach and I would have eaten anything. Between two slices of toasted wheat bread were spinach leaves and tuna salad. I felt too thankful to complain, and closed my faux eyelashed eyes as I bit into the moist sandwich. I made a mental note never to knock tuna again, and I learned a very important lesson: Always pack a lunch.

TUNA SALAD
MADRILEÑO

Prep Time: *10 minutes*
Cook Time: *None*

One 6-ounce can solid white
  tuna packed in spring water,
  drained

5 teaspoons light mayonnaise

1 tablespoon minced pimiento

1 tablespoon snipped fresh dill,
  or ½ teaspoon dried dill

6 to 8 drops hot pepper sauce,
  or to taste

Fresh lemon juice to taste

Salt and freshly ground black pepper
  to taste

4 cups crisp spinach leaves or salad
  greens, as an accompaniment

4 slices wheat toast

1. In a bowl combine the tuna, mayonnaise, pimiento, dill, hot pepper
sauce, lemon juice, salt, and pepper.

2. Arrange spinach and salad greens on two serving plates and divide tuna
salad between them. Serve with wheat toast.

Serves 2.

(Per serving) Calories: 142; Protein: 25g; Fat: 2g;
Carbohydrates: 6g; Cholesterol: 31mg; Sodium: 426mg.

There is no love sincerer than the love of food.

—*George Bernard Shaw*

CHICK-PEAS AND SPINACH TAPAS

This was originally served as a tapas snack, but I usually wound up standing by the bar and finishing a whole dish served for everyone to nibble from. So now I make it at home as a whole meal. It's great to serve with toasted bread or stuff into pita pockets.

Prep Time: 10 minutes
Cook Time: 8 to 10 minutes (for spinach)

10 ounces fresh spinach leaves, rinsed, or one 10-ounce package frozen leaf spinach

19-ounce can (2 cups) chick-peas, drained and rinsed

1 red bell pepper, finely diced

1 tablespoon snipped fresh chives

Juice of 1 to 2 lemons, or to taste

1/4 to 1/3 cup extra-virgin olive oil

Salt and freshly ground black pepper to taste

1. If using fresh spinach: Cook the spinach in a saucepan with the water clinging to its leaves, stirring, until wilted. Drain, squeeze dry, and finely chop. If using frozen spinach, follow package directions, drain, squeeze dry, and finely chop.

2. In a bowl combine the spinach with the chick-peas, pepper, chives, lemon juice, oil, salt, and pepper. Serve as is or chilled with toasted bread or as a filling for pita pockets.

Serves 4.

(Per serving) Calories: 280; Protein: 7g; Fat: 15g; Carbohydrates: 30g; Cholesterol: 0mg; Sodium: 400mg.

Cooking is a way of giving and making yourself desirable.

—*Charles Dudley Warner*

> There is never any ending to Paris and the memory of each person who has lived in it differs from that of any other. We always returned to it no matter who we were or how it was changed or with what difficulties, or ease, it could be reached. Paris was always worth it and you received return for whatever you brought to it.
>
> —*Ernest Hemingway*

Each of us has a charmed part of our lives we remember with nostalgia as a carefree and idealistic time. For me it is when I was in Paris that cold winter of my first year as a model.

I had little money and was taken in by Michael, a former professor who was on sabbatical. I had just started modeling. To go from grueling castings where there were dozens of girls like me fighting for the same job to Michael's relaxed living room to drink wine, eat wonderful meals, and share in discussion with the most varied cast of characters was a dream come true. I must admit my work did little to stimulate me. But Michael's home on rue d'Alesia became a den I pictured Gertrude Stein might have had. All those bohemian intellectuals who doted on me (I suppose as an amusement), but one who could cook well enough to earn her place at their table. Those evenings made it possible to get up the next day and battle for myself again.

There were all sorts of discoveries, small and large, that I made on a weekly basis. Soon I began to know my way around Paris and my way around modeling as well. I can hear Tom Waits in the background and the sound of Michael chopping the onions as I slam the door on another day's round of castings. Where's my apron?

F
R
A
N
C
E

PARISIAN CHICKEN SALAD

Most of us think of French food as quite fattening, and indeed it can tend to get rather heavy. Yet I found this chicken salad to be lighter than normal Parisian fare and realized it was the preparation of the chicken that rendered the flavor of the dish.

Prep Time: *20 minutes*

Cook Time: *10 minutes*

4 cups mixed baby greens,
  rinsed and patted dry

1 cup sliced mushrooms

1 cup diced fennel

1 cup julienned carrots

1 cup diced celery

One 14-ounce can baby artichokes,
  drained and quartered

1 cup Calamata or Niçoise olives

½ cup thinly sliced scallion

1 whole boneless, skinless chicken
  breast, cut into halves and pounded
  to ½ inch thick

1 tablespoon minced fresh thyme
  leaves, or 1 teaspoon dried
  thyme, crumbled

Salt and freshly ground pepper
  to taste

1 tablespoon olive oil

½ cup dry white wine

½ cup canned chicken broth

1 to 2 teaspoons Dijon mustard,
  or to taste

For the dressing:

2 to 3 tablespoons olive oil, or to taste

1 tablespoon Balsamic vinegar

1. In a large salad bowl combine the greens, mushrooms, fennel, carrots, celery, artichokes, olives, and scallion, and toss the mixture to combine.*

2. Pat the chicken dry and season with the thyme, salt, and pepper.

3. In a large nonstick skillet set over moderately high heat, warm the oil until hot, add the chicken, and sauté it for 2 minutes. Turn and cook for 1 minute more. Transfer the chicken to a plate.

4. Add the wine to the skillet and reduce it by half. Add the broth, whisk in the mustard, and return the chicken to the skillet. Simmer 2 to 3 minutes, or until chicken is cooked through and springy to the touch.

5. Transfer the chicken to a plate, reduce the remaining liquid to ½ cup, and pour it into a small bowl.

6. **Make the dressing:** Add the olive oil, whisking, to the bowl of reduced cooking liquid and whisk in the vinegar and salt and pepper to taste.

7. Cut chicken into slices and add to the salad bowl. Pour juices from plate into dressing, whisking to combine, and drizzle over salad. Toss mixture until chicken and vegetables are well coated with dressing.

Serves 4 generously.

  *Prep time can be halved if precut vegetables are purchased in the fresh
  produce section of the supermarket.

(Per serving) Calories: 227; Protein: 18g; Fat: 9g;
Carbohydrates: 15g; Cholesterol: 37mg; Sodium: 650mg.

HONEYED
CHICKEN LEGS

Prep Time: *15 minutes*
Cook Time: *65 to 70 minutes*

6 whole chicken legs, skinned

4 carrots, sliced thick

1 large onion, cut into eighths

1 navel orange, cut into eighths

1 tablespoon Herbes de Provence

1 teaspoon seasoned salt or
  Cavender's Greek seasoning

2 tablespoons honey

1 tablespoon Dijon mustard

2 tablespoons olive oil,
  or to taste

Tabasco to taste

2 zucchini, sliced

FRANCE

14

1. Preheat oven to 350°F.

2. Arrange chicken in an oiled baking dish and surround with the carrots, onion and orange. Sprinkle the chicken and vegetables with the Herbes de Provence and seasoned salt.

3. In a small bowl combine the honey and mustard and brush the mixture over the chicken. Drizzle the chicken and vegetables with the oil and sprinkle with Tabasco. Bake, covered with foil, basting occasionally, for 45 minutes. Uncover, add zucchini, and bake for an additional 20 minutes, or until juices from chicken run clear and vegetables are tender. If desired, run under a preheated broiler about 4 inches from the heat until golden.

Serves 4.

(Per serving) Calories: 412; Protein: 45g; Fat: 15g;
Carbohydrates: 23g; Cholesterol: 170mg; Sodium: 256mg.

SAUTÉED STEAK IN RED WINE AND SHALLOT SAUCE

Prep Time: *10 minutes*

Cook Time: *10 to 12 minutes*

3 cups cauliflower florets

3 tablespoons minced shallots

1 tablespoon olive oil

Two 6-ounce filet mignon or
   sirloin steaks, each cut 1½
   to 2 inches thick, patted dry

Salt and freshly ground pepper
   to taste

½ cup dry red wine

½ cup canned beef broth

1 tablespoon unsalted butter

1. In a steamer, cook the cauliflower, covered, for 6 to 8 minutes, or until tender.

2. Meanwhile, prepare the steak. In a nonstick skillet set over moderately high heat, cook the shallots in the oil, stirring, for 2 minutes, or until softened. Season the steaks with salt and pepper, then add them to the skillet. Cook 4 to 5 minutes on each side for rare meat. Transfer the steaks to a plate and keep warm.

3. Add the wine to the skillet and reduce by half. Add the broth and simmer 1 to 2 minutes, or until flavorful. Swirl in the butter until melted.

4. Arrange the steak and cauliflower on two serving plates and spoon the sauce over the meat.

Serves 2.

(Per serving) Calories: 381; Protein: 40g; Fat: 15g;
Carbohydrates: 11g; Cholesterol: 120mg; Sodium: 576mg.

SALADE NIÇOISE

Prep Time: 20 minutes

Cook Time: 10 minutes

2 cups trimmed *haricots verts*
  or green beans

2 cups 1-inch diced potato

10 ounces mesclun,
  or mixed baby greens

1 cup julienned or shredded carrot

1 cup sliced radish

2 cups (two 6-ounce cans) solid white
  tuna in spring water, drained

1 cup Niçoise or similar black olives

The whites of 4 hard-boiled eggs,
  chopped, if desired

For the dressing:

2 tablespoons Dijon mustard

2 tablespoons Balsamic vinegar

1 tablespoon mayonnaise

Salt and freshly ground pepper to taste

3 tablespoons olive oil, or to taste

3 tablespoons minced fresh herbs, such
  as tarragon, chives, basil, dill or a
  combination, or 1 teaspoon Herbes
  de Provence

1. To a large saucepan of boiling salted water, add the green beans and potato and cook over moderately high heat for 6 minutes, or until just tender. Drain in a colander, rinse under cold running water, and pat dry.

2. Arrange the salad ingredients on serving plates.

3. **Make the dressing:** In a small bowl whisk together the mustard, vinegar, mayonnaise, salt, and pepper. Add the oil, in a stream, whisking, until the dressing is combined well. Whisk in the herbs.

4. Spoon the dressing over the salad. Serve with crusty bread, grilled or toasted.

Serves 4 to 6.

(Per serving) Calories: 271; Protein: 20g; Fat: 12g;
Carbohydrates: 21g; Cholesterol: 18mg; Sodium: 545mg.

Of all the items on the menu, soup is that which exacts the most delicate amount of perfection and the strictest attention.

—*Auguste Escoffier*

To me there's nothing more comforting than a bowl of warm soup. Countless colds have been melted away by the warm nourishment of a hearty stew. When preparing a soup, I never plan ahead, for the making of a pot of soup is an event. The joy is never knowing exactly how it will turn out. It doesn't take so much to build a good soup. A few potatoes, several zucchini, a few herbs, and bouillon cube can feed the most finicky diners. And a soup is truly made of its parts. The goodness lies in the graceful freshness and quality that make soup such a noble creation.

Quite by accident, I discovered a tiny restaurant near Rue Danielle Casanova in Paris not far from the Place Vendôme. I was coming from my agency and I was extremely upset that a job for French *Glamour* had just been canceled. My hands were frozen as I opened the door to a restaurant with almost no lighting. As my eyes adjusted to the dimness, I sat quietly consoling myself at one of the side tables. A slim French woman in her forties wearing too much makeup came to take my order. In my broken French, I tried to explain that I didn't have a menu, when she pointed to a small chalkboard over the door. I ordered a glass of red wine and attempted to decipher what I could of the French scrawl. I couldn't find anything I recognized and after an unsuccessful conversation filled with sign language and impatient sighs on her part, I suddenly began to cry. It seems now that I overreacted, it was ridiculous to get so worked up over one job, but I had really looked forward to what would have been quite a prestigious photo shoot for me.

My tears must have alarmed her. After a moment of dead silence, she disappeared into the kitchen. Soon after a man emerged from the kitchen, bringing me a glass of Cabernet. "Drink," he said. I took a few sips of wine and was warming up. I took off my coat and scarf and put my portfolio on the other chair across from me. After I had almost drained the glass this old, lanky man in the greasiest, dirtiest apron pulled up the chair across from me and sat down. He looked at me with kindly eyes and said, "What is so wrong to make such a sweet face so sad? You don't like our menu?"

"No," I said, "I just can't read it. It's not the menu, I've had a bad day. I just want some soup. Do you have any soup?"

"I have the greatest soup in Paris for you! But why do you cry? You are one of those mannequins from that Ford agency, *oui*? Drink," he commanded, "and wait." With that, he was off into the kitchen. After I had a few more sips of wine, the old man returned with a steaming tureen of what looked like a carrot purée. "This soup is a great favorite," he beamed. "All the mannequins love this soup, and you know, you girls don't like to eat very much." He stood there until I took the spoon and tried it, waiting for confirmation of its goodness. And it *was* good. By the time I was done with half of it he had taken the seat across from me with my portfolio in his hand. "This is your book? I can see it?" I had almost forgotten about the day's events, and resented his bringing them back to my memory. He must have seen my expression, for he quickly asked, "You like more soup? Don't worry, no charge for more, I only know to make always too much. Madeleine," he yelled, *"un autre crème de carotte."*

The skinny waitress came out with another, larger tureen in one hand and a cigarette hanging from the other. She stuck the cigarette in her mouth and put the soup on the table. She quickly replaced the ladle into the new batch and disappeared in a flash with the empty tureen.

"My daughter is jealous, so don't mind her. She thinks that I should speak only to my carrots and courgettes all day. How can I do this with all of you ladies waiting for me! So now, tell me, why do you cry? Is it a boyfriend, you girls are always crying about boyfriends?"

"No." I sniffled. "I just thought I was working tomorrow for a really big job, and . . . and . . . and . . ." I stuttered. It all seemed too silly even to me.

"Let's see, the pictures are very nice, maybe just rearrange them, put them, you know, in a different order. It is like when I make a soup. For example, in a potage aux légumes I cannot put the potato after the courgette because the potato takes longer to cook. In your soup also, everything has its time and place, otherwise . . ."

Phillippe the soup maker was now involved in placing photos of me on the back table and every two or three minutes I'd hear some muttering in French. My mood started to improve as I was getting full on bowl after bowl of this soup. Perhaps it was the wine as well. Phillippe, the splattered chef, knew what he was talking about when it came to soup. Since then I have often taken Phillippe's advice on how to arrange my photos, advice that was always easier to get than his recipes. I always felt there was one key addition missing from each of his recited ingredient lists, but I could never pin him down on the matter. But he is right in making me apply myself, so that "The soup will know who is the chef!" So I took his advice and added some grated ginger to my version.

POTAGE AUX LÉGUMES

Prep Time: 15 minutes

Cook Time: 30 minutes

2 tablespoons olive oil

1 large onion, thinly sliced

4 carrots, thinly sliced

4 celery stalks, thinly sliced

½ fennel bulb, thinly sliced

Salt and freshly ground black
    pepper to taste

1½ pounds zucchini, sliced

4 potatoes, sliced

5 cups broccoli florets

A sprig fresh thyme, or 1 teaspoon
    dried thyme, crumbled

1 large bay leaf

¼ cup chopped fresh parsley

10 cups water

2 Knorr chicken bouillon cubes

½ teaspoon Cavender's Greek
    Seasoning, if available

Pistou (see following recipe)

1. In a casserole set over moderate heat, warm the oil until it is hot, add the onion, carrots, celery, fennel, and salt and pepper, and cook the mixture, stirring occasionally, for 5 minutes. Add the zucchini, potatoes, and broccoli florets, and continue to cook the vegetables for 3 minutes more. Add the thyme, bay leaf, parsley, water, bouillon cubes, Cavender's Seasoning, and salt and pepper to taste. Bring to a boil and simmer, partially covered, stirring occasionally, for 20 minutes, or until vegetables are tender. Remove and discard the thyme sprig and bay leaf.

2. Transfer the soup, in batches, to a blender or food processor and blend until smooth. Return to casserole and simmer over moderate heat, stirring occasionally, until heated through.

3. Serve Pistou on the side, or garnish each serving with a tablespoon of the pistou.

Makes about 16 cups, serving 8 to 10.

(Per serving) Calories: 175; Protein: 7g; Fat: 4g;
Carbohydrates: 31g; Cholesterol: 0mg; Sodium: 347mg.

PISTOU

Prep Time: 15 minutes
Cook Time: None

4 garlic cloves, mashed
   to a paste
2 cups fresh basil leaves
1 cup freshly grated Parmesan

Freshly ground black pepper
¾ to 1 cup extra-virgin
   olive oil
Salt to taste

In a food processor or blender combine the garlic, basil, Parmesan, and pepper. With the machine running, add the oil in a stream and process until combined to a paste. Add salt to taste.

Makes about 1⅓ cups.

(Per serving) Calories: 95; Protein: 2g; Fat: 9g;
Carbohydrates: 1g; Cholesterol: 3mg; Sodium: 75mg.

**A cook is creative, marrying ingredients
in the way a poet marries words.**

—Roger Verge

CRÈME DE CAROTTE

CARROT SOUP

Prep Time: *10 minutes*
Cook Time: *20 to 25 minutes*

5 large (about 1¼ pounds)
   carrots, sliced

1 potato, sliced

½ teaspoon minced gingerroot,
   or to taste

8 cups water

2 Knorr chicken bouillon cubes

Salt to taste

2 to 3 tablespoons snipped fresh dill

Nonfat plain yogurt as a garnish,
   if desired

1. In a large saucepan or casserole set over moderately high heat combine the carrots, potato, ginger, water, bouillon cubes, and salt. Bring to a boil and simmer, covered, for 15 to 20 minutes, or until carrots are tender.

2. In a food processor or blender purée the soup in batches and return to pan. Reheat until hot, stir in the dill, and garnish with the yogurt.

Makes 8 cups, serving 4 to 6.

(Per serving) Calories: 65; Protein: 2g; Fat: 1g;
Carbohydrates: 14g; Cholesterol: 0mg; Sodium: 471mg.

To make good soup, the pot must only simmer or smile.

—French Proverb

PROVENÇALE TOMATO-POTATO STEW

Prep Time: *15 minutes*
Cook Time: *25 minutes*

2 tablespoons olive oil

4 large cloves garlic, finely minced, or to taste

2 pounds firm, ripe tomatoes, cored and cut into 1-inch pieces

2 pounds (about 3 large) potatoes, peeled and cut into 1-inch pieces

Salt and freshly ground black pepper

6 to 7 cups water

2 Knorr chicken bouillon cubes

3 sprigs fresh rosemary, or 1½ teaspoons dried, crumbled

2 bay leaves

1 tablespoon minced fresh oregano, or 1½ teaspoons dried, crumbled

1 teaspoon Herbes de Provence

1 teaspoon lemon pepper seasoning

3 dried red chilies, or to taste (optional)

⅓ cup minced fresh parsley

Lemon juice to taste

FRANCE

◆

24

In a large saucepan or casserole set over moderate heat, warm the oil until hot, add the garlic, and cook, stirring, 1 minute. Add the tomatoes, potatoes, and salt and pepper, and cook, stirring occasionally, for 5 minutes. Add enough water to cover the vegetables, the bouillon cubes, herbs, lemon pepper, and chilies. Add salt and pepper to taste, bring to a boil, and simmer, skimming and stirring occasionally, for 15 minutes, or until vegetables are tender. Before serving discard bay leaves and rosemary sprigs, stir in the parsley, and season with the lemon juice.

Serves 4 to 6

(Per serving) Calories: 159; Protein: 4g; Fat: 5g; Carbohydrates: 26g; Cholesterol: 0mg; Sodium: 472mg.

CRÈME DE COURGETTE

ZUCCHINI SOUP

Prep Time: *15 minutes*
Cook Time: *30 minutes*

1 onion, chopped

2 small carrots, chopped

1 tablespoon minced garlic

2 tablespoons olive oil

2 potatoes, sliced

4 medium-large zucchini, sliced

1 tablespoon minced fresh thyme,
  or 1 teaspoon dried thyme

1 teaspoon minced gingerroot

½ teaspoon Cavender's Greek
  seasoning, if available

¼ teaspoon crushed red pepper flakes,
  or to taste

Salt and freshly ground black pepper
  to taste

Water to cover

3 Knorr chicken bouillon cubes

Fresh lemon juice to taste

1. In a casserole set over moderate heat, cook the onion, carrots, and garlic in the olive oil, covered, stirring occasionally, for 5 minutes. Add the potatoes and zucchini and cook, stirring, 3 minutes more. Add the thyme, gingerroot, Greek seasoning, red pepper flakes, salt, and pepper, and stir to combine. Add enough water to cover and the bouillon cubes, bring to a boil, and simmer, partially covered, stirring occasionally, for 20 minutes, or until vegetables are tender.

2. In a food processor or blender, purée the soup, in batches, and return to the pan. Reheat until hot. Correct seasoning, adding more salt, pepper, and fresh lemon juice to taste.

Serves 6 to 8

(Per serving) Calories: 92; Protein: 2g; Fat: 3g;
Carbohydrates: 13g; Cholesterol: 0mg; Sodium: 454mg.

THREE-BEAN SOUP

Prep Time: 15 minutes

Cook Time: 30 to 35 minutes

1 tablespoon olive oil

1 onion, minced

3 cloves garlic, smashed and peeled

4 small carrots, sliced

1 bell pepper, cut into 1-inch pieces

Salt and freshly ground black pepper
    to taste

6 large tomatoes, cored and cut into
    1-inch pieces

1 tablespoon minced fresh oregano, or
    1 teaspoon dried oregano, crumbled

1 teaspoon Herbes de Provence

$^{1}/_{2}$ teaspoon Cavender's Greek
    seasoning, if available

5 cups water

3 Knorr chicken bouillon cubes

One 12-ounce can chick-peas,
    drained and rinsed

One 12-ounce can kidney beans,
    drained and rinsed

One 12-ounce can cannellini beans,
    drained and rinsed

$^{1}/_{4}$ cup minced fresh parsley

Fresh lemon juice to taste

In a casserole or large saucepan set over moderate heat, warm the oil until it
is hot, add the onion, garlic, carrots, bell pepper, salt, and pepper, and cook
the mixture, stirring occasionally, for 5 to 7 minutes, or until vegetables are
softened. Add the tomatoes, oregano, Herbes de Provence, and Greek seasoning, and simmer, stirring, 5 minutes more. Add the water, bouillon
cubes, and more salt and pepper to taste, bring to a boil, stirring, and simmer 10 minutes. Add the beans and simmer 5 minutes more, or until
heated through. Before serving stir in the parsley and lemon juice.

Makes 10 cups, serving 6.

(Per serving) Calories: 428; Protein: 23g; Fat: 4g;
Carbohydrates: 78g; Cholesterol: 0mg; Sodium: 1054mg.

> Cooking is like love. It should be entered
> into with abandon or not at all.
>
> —*Harriet Van Horn*

I would be hard pressed to choose which part of Italy is my favorite, but I am partial to my neighborhood in the center of Milan called Brera. After working in all parts of the world it is nice to come back to where I am thought of as a local. There are many beautiful places in Italy, but what I will always love most are its people. My love of this culture has a lot to do with the food. The Mediterranean diet has always appealed to me, even the hearty risottos and osso buco from Northern Italy. The precept that any good celebration is nothing without the preparation of fine food and drink is nowhere truer than in Italy, and Italians seem to have a celebratory nature inherent in their culture. When I first gave a few dinners for friends at home I had a tendency to overdo things. Then I began to notice that other hosts and even restaurants served much simpler fare than the elaborate concoctions I was preparing. I slowly learned that one main dish made with wholesome ingredients and lots of care is better than a table full of warring flavors. I learned to give food an importance that is simple and honest. Being in Italy showed me the refined joy that comes from a simple bowl of tomato soup and good crusty bread.

I am never so happy as when I am cooking for someone I love. But the joy of cooking can unfortunately be diminished by the ignorant demands of those who do not understand that to compromise in the kitchen is a great sin. Daniele, my former partner, got it into his head that he needed to go into food detoxification. He decided that my cooking was too exciting for his system. One November night I suggested we dine at home. He said he'd be happy to eat something simple prepared at home. "Something simple," I soon realized, meant rice and vegetables boiled to a watery death. He saw my face when the pathetic meal was before me and said he'd wanted to "clean out his system," that it needed a rest. He liked to eat light and said that as a model I should want to do the same since I wasn't going to be young forever. A knife stabbed slowly through my heart.

I
T
A
L
Y

And after that sorry meal, he started saying that rice was very good for one's constitution. Was he trying to teach a girl from India the virtues of rice? He began to require a weekly regimen of one or two dinners with rice. All of a sudden it was like being home again with Mom. Rice, rice, and more rice.

To his credit, he was right about eating a well-tempered diet. I too felt better when I didn't eat fried or cream-filled foods, but this obsession with vegetables and rice came suddenly and, as far as I could tell, out of nowhere. I thought this was some hidden test Italian men put their women through. At first, I simply bought an array of varied vegetables at the local outdoor market. An Italian farmers' market is one of my favorite places to pass a free afternoon. I started bringing home whatever strange flora the *fruttivendolo* recommended. I began to boil them for less time with less water so the natural flavor of the vegetable was still intact. Then I began steaming slightly with very little water. Slowly, month by month, I worked Daniele to my side of the kitchen, compromising for my own health and that of our cohabitation. When contemplating our future together, it became clear that I would always have to contend with his tyranny at the table. I was in love with a food fascist. Slowly, he confessed that onions, garlic, and a list of other ingredients made his stomach uneasy. He showed me the little empty plastic packets of Maalox in his pocket, which gave me a prompt attack of guilt. So, since he was safe with rice (at least psychologically), I started creating recipes that were light, yet tastier than the dull hospital-type food he had resigned himself to. There was more harmony in our home as well as in Daniele's stomach. After coming home from shoots in Mexico or Jamaica, I was tired of all the greasy hotel food and looked forward to a bowl of rice either with some beans or bathed in a mushroom broth. And I admit having rice frequently did make me feel a bit more at home. I started sneaking a bit of cumin and other spices into the rice dishes, and it became quite a game to see how much I could get away with without hearing protests from the food police.

LUCA'S LENTILS

In Italy it is tradition to eat lentils at New Year's celebrations to ensure prosperity. The more lentils eaten, the more success is said to befall the diner, the lentils being a sort of gastronomic symbol for money or coinage. My friend Luca Orlandi, who is a young designer working in New York, is doing quite well, and I take unashamed partial credit that this is because he loves my lentils. Once he reminisced about the bowls of hot lentils his mother would make him during his youth in the winter months of Northern Italy. Being busy in New York opening up stores has kept him away from the cuisine he can only find near the mountains and lakes of his hometown region. To celebrate the opening of his second store on Madison Avenue, I prepared this dish for him.

Prep Time: 10 minutes
Cook Time: 25 to 30 minutes

1 tablespoon olive oil

1 small onion, minced

1 carrot, diced

Salt and freshly ground black
    pepper to taste

2 cloves garlic, peeled and smashed

3 tomatoes, cored and diced

1 teaspoon minced fresh gingerroot

1/2 teaspoon hot or medium Madras
    curry powder or Garam Masala

1/2 teaspoon lemon pepper seasoning

1/2 teaspoon Herbes de Provence

2 bay leaves

1 cup water

1 Knorr chicken bouillon cube

4 cups precooked brown lentils

1 to 2 tablespoons fresh lemon juice,
    or to taste

Extra-virgin olive oil for drizzling

1. In a large saucepan set over moderate heat, warm the oil until it is hot, add the onion, carrot, salt, and pepper, and cook, stirring occasionally, for 5 minutes. Add the garlic and cook 1 minute. Add the tomatoes, gingerroot, curry powder or Garam Masala, lemon pepper seasoning, Herbes de Provence, and bay leaves, and cook, stirring occasionally, for 2 minutes. Add the water and bouillon cube and cook, stirring occasionally, for 5 to 7 minutes more, or until mixture has thickened. Add the lentils, and simmer, stirring occasionally, for 5 to 7 minutes more, or until flavors have blended. Discard bay leaves.

2. Before serving, stir in the lemon juice and drizzle with the extra-virgin olive oil.

Serves 4.

**(Per serving) Calories: 318; Protein: 19g; Fat: 4g;
Carbohydrates: 53g; Cholesterol: 0mg; Sodium: 353mg.**

CARPACCIO DI PESCE

This recipe was given to me by a sweet man named Renato who calls it Italian sushi. Renato is an old family friend of Daniele's parents from Como in Northern Italy and is a master in the kitchen. I first met Renato while spending the weekend in Sardegna. I love Sardegna, with its still, clear sea. It remains one of the favorite places to sneak away to in early summer. One day we went out on a boat, and after snorkeling and swimming the whole afternoon, we became pretty famished. Renato brought out this dish and served it with some warm bread. We descended on the platter like seagulls and watched the sun set over the Mediterranean.

Prep Time: 20 minutes,
            including marinating
Cook Time: None

1 pound fish fillets, such as trout
   or sea bass

Juice of 2 lemons

1 tablespoon olive oil, or to taste

1 tablespoon capers, minced

1 tablespoon whole red peppercorns,
   lightly crushed

Salt to taste

Minced fresh parsley leaves to taste

Grilled bread as an accompaniment

1. Place fish in freezer for 10 minutes to facilitate cutting. With a very sharp knife, cut the fillets into paper thin slices and arrange on a serving plate.

2. In a small bowl whisk together the lemon juice and olive oil. Drizzle the dressing over the fish and sprinkle with the capers and peppercorns. Season with the salt. Let sit for 5 minutes and sprinkle with the parsley. Serve with the bread.

Serves 4.

(Per serving) Calories: 199; Protein: 24g; Fat: 10g;
Carbohydrates: 1g; Cholesterol: 66mg; Sodium: 78mg.

PENNE ALL' ARRABBIATA

PENNE WITH SPICY TOMATO SAUCE

Prep Time: 10 minutes
Cook Time: 12 to 15 minutes

1 pound penne

3 tablespoons olive oil

4 cloves garlic, peeled and smashed

1 large, not very ripe, fresh tomato, cored and diced

2 small bay leaves

1 1/2 teaspoons minced fresh oregano, or 1/2 teaspoon dried oregano, crumbled

One 28-ounce can crushed tomatoes in purée

1 Knorr chicken or beef bouillon cube, crumbled

2 teaspoons dried red pepper flakes, or to taste

1/2 teaspoon sugar

Fresh basil to taste

Freshly grated Parmesan as an accompaniment

1. In a large pot of boiling salted water, cook the penne according to package directions. Drain.

2. Meanwhile, in a sauté pan or deep skillet set over moderate heat, warm the oil until it is hot, add the garlic, and cook it, stirring, until golden. Add the tomato and cook for 2 to 3 minutes. Add the bay leaves, oregano, crushed tomatoes, bouillon, red pepper flakes, and sugar, bring to a boil, and simmer, stirring frequently, for 10 minutes. Remove and discard the garlic and bay leaves. Stir in the basil.

3. In a large bowl combine the pasta and sauce and toss until pasta is completely coated with sauce. Serve with Parmesan to taste.

Serves 6.

(Per serving) Calories: 608; Protein: 18g; Fat: 12g; Carbohydrates: 107g; Cholesterol: 0mg; Sodium: 1377mg.

CANNELLINI RICE

Prep Time: *10 minutes*
Cook Time: *15 to 20 minutes*

2 tablespoons olive oil

½ onion, finely chopped

1 green bell pepper,
  finely chopped

3 cloves garlic, peeled
  but left whole

4 tomatoes, coarsely chopped

2 bay leaves

1 teaspoon dried oregano,
  crumbled

1 teaspoon Italian seasoning

1 teaspoon lemon pepper

1 Knorr chicken, beef,
  or vegetable bouillon cube

1 cup boiling water

4 cups cooked rice

A 15-ounce can cannellini
  beans, drained and rinsed

Salt to taste

Extra-virgin olive oil to taste

Freshly grated Parmesan
  to taste

1. In a deep skillet or sauté pan set over moderate heat, warm the oil until it is hot. Add the onion, green pepper, and garlic, and cook the mixture, stirring occasionally, for 5 minutes, or until softened. Add the tomatoes, bay leaves, oregano, Italian seasoning, and lemon pepper, and cook the mixture 1 minute. Dissolve the bouillon in the water, add to the tomato mixture and simmer, stirring occasionally, for 10 minutes.

2. Add the rice, cannellini beans, and salt, and simmer the mixture, stirring occasionally, for 5 minutes more, or until beans and rice are heated through. Mixture will have the consistency of a risotto. Remove and discard bay leaves. Season with the olive oil and sprinkle with cheese to taste.

Serves 4 to 6.

(Per serving) **Calories: 490; Protein: 21g; Fat: 5g;**
Carbohydrates: 89g; Cholesterol: 0mg; Sodium: 322mg.

On the Couch with Gretha

It's quite difficult to keep up friendships in modeling. All of us travel so much and the only time we get together is during the shows. Occasionally, I do get to see some friends regularly. Once my friend Gretha, a model from Bologna, Italy, stayed with me for four months in my New York apartment. It was great to have her company, someone to cook and share meals with. Gretha eats like a baby, she likes very mild food, barely spiced, and plain as possible. But being Italian, she also loves good food. In my small apartment, overlooking the East River, we polished off bowl after bowl of Fiery Farfalle or Rigatoni al Pomodoro. I think we both longed for Italy. Over pasta we have cried, laughed, and grumbled about everything from work to men to our mothers. Gretha is usually reserved and shy when it comes to showing her emotions. I secretly believe it was my bowls of steaming pasta night after night that made her begin to confide in me. She still complains from time to time about my heavy hand with red pepper, but no friendship is perfect.

GRETHA'S BASIC SPAGHETTI SAUCE

Prep Time: 10 minutes

Cook Time: 12 to 15 minutes

1 pound spaghetti

2 tablespoons olive oil

3 cloves garlic,
  peeled and smashed

One 28-ounce can crushed
  tomatoes in purée

3 small bay leaves

1½ tablespoons minced fresh
  oregano, or 2 teaspoons dried
  oregano, crumbled

1 Knorr chicken or beef bouillon
  cube, crumbled

6 sun-dried tomatoes packed
  in oil, drained and minced

½ teaspoon lemon pepper
  seasoning

3 tablespoons minced fresh basil

Freshly grated Parmesan as an
  accompaniment

1. In a large pot of boiling salted water, cook the spaghetti according to package directions. Drain.

2. Meanwhile, in a sauté pan or deep skillet set over moderate heat, warm the oil until it is hot, add the garlic, and cook it, stirring, until golden. Add the tomatoes, bay leaves, oregano, bouillon, sun-dried tomatoes, and lemon pepper, and simmer the sauce stirring occasionally, for 10 minutes. Remove and discard garlic and bay leaves. Stir in the basil.

3. In a large bowl combine the pasta and sauce and toss until pasta is completely coated with sauce. Serve with Parmesan to taste.

Serves 4.

(Per serving) Calories: 221; Protein: 9g; Fat: 6g;
Carbohydrates: 39g; Cholesterol: 0mg; Sodium: 1635mg.

MANICOTTI MAGRI

VEAL-FILLED PASTA WITH TOMATO SAUCE

Prep Time: *15 minutes*
Cook Time: *25 to 30 minutes*

12 Manicotti tubes (about 8 ounces)

1 tablespoon olive oil

1 onion, minced

10 ounces ground veal or turkey

1 teaspoon lemon pepper

2 to 3 teaspoons minced fresh
  oregano, or 1 teaspoon dried
  oregano, crumbled

Salt and freshly ground black pepper
  to taste

3 tablespoons minced fresh parsley

1/4 cup minced drained sun-dried
  tomatoes in oil

1 pound part-skim ricotta

1/3 cup freshly grated Parmesan

3 cups Gretha's Basic Spaghetti Sauce
  or store-bought marinara sauce

1. Preheat the oven to 350°F.

2. In a large pot of boiling, salted water, cook the Manicotti tubes according to package directions. Drain, rinse in cold water, and pat dry.

3. In a nonstick skillet set over moderate heat, warm the oil until hot. Add the onion and cook it, stirring occasionally, for 5 minutes. Add the meat, lemon pepper, oregano, salt, and pepper, and cook, stirring, until the meat is no longer pink.

4. Transfer the meat to a bowl, add the parsley, tomatoes, ricotta, and half the Parmesan, and fill the pasta tubes with the meat mixture.

5. Spoon 1 cup sauce in bottom of shallow baking dish, top with the filled pasta tubes, and spoon the remaining sauce over them. Sprinkle with the remaining Parmesan and bake for 25 to 30 minutes, or until sauce is bubbling.

Serves 4 to 6.

(Per serving) Calories: 403; Protein: 24g; Fat: 14g;
Carbohydrates: 46g; Cholesterol: 44mg; Sodium: 1055mg.

PORTO WINE PASTA

PASTA IN PORT WINE AND MUSHROOM SAUCE

Prep Time: *10 minutes*
Cook Time: *20 to 25 minutes*

1 pound fettuccine

2 tablespoons olive oil

1 cup minced onion

½ pound Portobello or white
   mushrooms, sliced

Salt and freshly ground black
   pepper to taste

½ teaspoon Herbes de Provence

½ teaspoon lemon pepper

1 cup port or red wine

½ cup canned beef broth

2 tablespoons minced fresh
   parsley leaves

1. In a large pot of boiling salted water, cook the fettuccine according to package directions and drain.

2. Meanwhile, make the sauce: In a large nonstick skillet set over moderate heat, warm the oil until hot. Add the onion and cook, stirring occasionally, 5 minutes. Add the mushrooms, salt, pepper, Herbes de Provence, and lemon pepper, and cook, stirring occasionally, for 5 minutes. Add the port and reduce 3 minutes. Add broth and simmer 2 minutes. Correct seasoning.

3. Add pasta to skillet, toss until coated with the sauce, and sprinkle with the parsley.

Serves 4.

(Per serving) **Calories:** 567; **Protein:** 16g; **Fat:** 9g;
Carbohydrates: 95g; **Cholesterol:** 0mg; **Sodium:** 259mg.

The kitchen is a country in which there
are always discoveries to be made.

—*Grimod de la Reyniere*

SPAGHETTI DI CAPRI

SPAGHETTI WITH FRESH TOMATOES, BLACK OLIVES, AND BASIL

Every summer there is a big swimwear fashion show done in the main piazza of Capri called ModaMare, shown on Italian television. Being careful of one's weight before a fashion show is normal practice, but the stakes are doubly high when you're in just a bathing suit on the runway. This dish made with freshly chopped cherry tomatoes is a great way to eat light. Somehow it always tastes better in Capri. Not only because of the ambiance but because the vegetables that grow in the Mediterranean sun and soil have a flavor that is all their own.

Prep Time: *15 minutes*
Cook Time: *8 to 10 minutes*

2 pounds cherry tomatoes, halved
  or quartered, depending upon size

1½ cups finely diced celery

1½ cups pitted black olives,
  such as Niçoise or Kalamata,
  halved if large

1 cup chopped fresh basil

1 teaspoon lemon pepper, or to taste

Salt

1 pound spaghetti

⅓ to ½ cup extra-virgin olive oil

1. Halve or quarter the tomatoes, depending on size, over a large bowl to catch all the juices. To the bowl with the tomatoes, add the celery, olives, basil, lemon pepper, and salt, and toss to combine.

2. In a large pot of boiling salted water cook the pasta according to package directions. Drain and transfer to the bowl.

3. Add the olive oil and salt to taste and toss to combine.

Serves 6.

(Per serving) Calories: 462; Protein: 12g; Fat: 15g;
Carbohydrates: 71g; Cholesterol: 0mg; Sodium: 200mg.

FIERY FARFALLE

SPICED BOW-TIE PASTA WITH RED, YELLOW, AND GREEN BELL PEPPERS

Prep Time: 15 minutes
Cook Time: 20 minutes

1 pound farfalle (bow-tie) pasta
1 tablespoon olive oil
1 onion, sliced thin
2 each green, red, and yellow
   peppers, thinly sliced
2 large cloves garlic, minced
1 tablespoon minced fresh oregano,
   or 1 teaspoon dried oregano,
   crumbled

½ teaspoon lemon pepper
1 bay leaf
¼ teaspoon red pepper flakes,
   or to taste
Salt to taste
1 Knorr chicken bouillon cube,
   crumbled
Freshly grated Parmesan
Italian bread

1. Fill a large pot or casserole with water and bring it to the boil over moderately high heat. Add salt and farfalle and cook pasta according to package directions.

2. Meanwhile, in a large nonstick skillet set over moderately high heat, warm the oil until hot. Add the onion and cook, stirring occasionally, for 5 minutes. Add the peppers, garlic, oregano, lemon pepper, bay leaf, dried red pepper flakes, and salt, and cook the mixture, stirring frequently, for 5 minutes more. Add 1½ to 2 cups hot water from pasta pot and the bouillon cube to the onion-pepper mixture, and simmer the sauce, stirring occasionally, for 8 to 10 minutes more, or until sauce is flavorful. Discard bay leaf.

3. Drain pasta and transfer to a large bowl. Add the sauce and toss to combine. Serve with freshly grated Parmesan and crusty Italian bread.

Serves 4 to 6.

(Per serving) Calories: 333; Protein: 10g; Fat: 3g;
Carbohydrates: 63g; Cholesterol: 0mg; Sodium: 228mg.

LASAGNA ROLLS

Prep Time: *25 minutes*
Cook Time: *35 to 45 minutes*

12 dried lasagna noodles

One 10-ounce package frozen
leaf spinach

15 to 16 ounces ricotta cheese

6 tablespoons freshly grated Parmesan

¼ cup minced drained sun-dried
tomatoes packed in oil

2 tablespoons minced black olives,
such as Kalamata

1 teaspoon dried Italian seasoning

½ teaspoon lemon pepper seasoning

¼ to ½ teaspoon dried red pepper
flakes, or to taste

Salt to taste

3 cups spaghetti or marinara sauce

1 tablespoon dried bread crumbs

Olive oil to taste

Basil sprigs for garnish

1. In a large pot of salted boiling water, cook the lasagna noodles according to package directions, drain, and rinse under cold water. Pat dry with paper towels.

2. Cook the spinach according to package directions, squeeze dry, and chop.

3. In a bowl combine the spinach, ricotta, 4 tablespoons of the Parmesan, the sun-dried tomatoes, black olives, Italian seasoning, lemon pepper, red pepper flakes, and salt to taste.

4. Working with one pasta noodle at a time, smooth an even layer of the filling down on each strip, then roll up to enclose filling. Prepare remaining rolls in the same manner.

5. Spoon a thin layer of sauce into a baking pan, top with the lasagna rolls, seam side down, and cover with the remaining sauce. Sprinkle top with the remaining 2 tablespoons of Parmesan and bread crumbs and drizzle with a little oil.

6. Bake in the oven for 35 to 45 minutes, or until bubbling. Garnish with the basil.

Serves 4 to 6.

(Per serving) Calories: 320; Protein: 18g; Fat: 8g;
Carbohydrates: 44g; Cholesterol: 25mg; Sodium: 1063mg.

PESCE SPADA

BAKED SWORDFISH WITH TOMATOES AND BASIL

Prep Time: *20 minutes, including marinating*
Cook Time: *12 to 15 minutes*

1 tablespoon olive oil

1 tablespoon lemon juice

1 tablespoon minced fresh oregano,
   or 1 teaspoon dried oregano,
   crumbled

2 cloves garlic, finely minced

Salt and freshly ground pepper to taste

Four 6-ounce swordfish* or similar fish
   steaks, such as mako shark or tuna,
   cut 1-inch thick

4 firm, ripe tomatoes, diced

2 tablespoons minced fresh basil

Lemon juice to taste

Lemon wedges as an accompaniment

1. Preheat oven to 350°F.

2. In a bowl whisk together the oil, lemon juice, oregano, garlic, and salt and pepper. In a shallow dish coat the fish steaks with the mixture and let marinate, covered and chilled, for 15 minutes.

3. Arrange the fish in a foil-lined baking pan and bake for 12 to 15 minutes, or until fish is just cooked.

4. In a bowl toss the tomatoes with the basil and salt and pepper to taste.

5. Transfer the fish to serving plates and top each with some of the tomato/basil salad. Sprinkle with lemon juice and garnish with lemon wedges.

Serves 4.

  *Since swordfish is now an endangered species, you may
  want to substitute some other firm-fleshed fish here.

**(Per serving) Calories: 283; Protein: 35g; Fat: 10g;
Carbohydrates: 11g; Cholesterol: 66mg; Sodium: 167mg.**

SPINACH AND BEEF SALAD

It was a small joy when I discovered fresh spinach could taste so good. I was doing a haute couture show on the Spanish Steps in Rome. The dresses were long and regal and extremely form-fitting. I had nightmarish visions of tumbling down the stairs, my long gown tearing as the little buttons popped one by one. So after my fitting, I decided to watch what I ate, something I wasn't very good at given my love for food. It was hot anyway and I didn't feel like having a big meal, so I went to this trattoria near Piazza di Spagna. I decided on the spinach salad even though it had meat in it. My Brahmin grandmother would probably disagree, but a girl in the world can't live on rice alone. Balsamic vinegar and spinach make an excellent combination, and this salad is a great summer dish.

Prep Time: 25 minutes,
            including marinating
Cook Time: 8 to 10 minutes

8 ounces sirloin or filet mignon
   steak, cut into strips
2 tablespoons soy sauce
1 tablespoon olive oil
1 teaspoon minced garlic
Freshly ground pepper to taste
8 ounces shiitake or similar
   wild mushroom, trimmed,
   wiped clean and sliced*
Salt to taste
12 ounces fresh spinach leaves,
   trimmed, rinsed, and patted dry

For the dressing:
4 tablespoons Balsamic vinegar,
   or to taste
1½ teaspoons Dijon mustard
2 to 3 teaspoons lemon pepper,
   or to taste
Salt to taste
4 tablespoons olive oil,
   or to taste
Minced fresh herbs, such as dill,
   chives, basil, or a combination

*White cultivated mushrooms may be substituted and do not need to be cooked.

1. In a bowl combine the steak, soy sauce, olive oil, garlic, and pepper. Let marinate 15 minutes.

2. Warm a nonstick skillet over moderately high heat until it is hot. Add the steak, marinade, and salt, and cook, stirring, just until the meat is no longer pink (be careful not to overcook). With a slotted spoon transfer the steak to a plate.

3. Add the remaining oil to the skillet and warm it over moderately high heat until hot. Add the mushrooms and salt and pepper, and cook, stirring, for 5 minutes.

4. In a salad bowl combine the steak, mushrooms along with any pan juices, and spinach leaves, tossing gently to combine.

5. **Make the dressing:** In a bowl whisk together the vinegar, mustard, lemon pepper, and salt to taste. Add the oil, in a stream, whisking until combined well. Whisk in the herbs.

6. Pour the dressing over the salad and toss to combine. Serve with grilled or toasted bread.

Serves 4 to 6.

(Per serving) **Calories:** 281; **Protein:** 13g; **Fat:** 13g; **Carbohydrates:** 31g; **Cholesterol:** 23mg; **Sodium:** 588mg.

All cooks, like all great artists, must have an audience worth cooking for.

—*Charles Dudley Warner*

POLLO ALLA CACCIATORE

Prep Time: 10 minutes
Cook Time: 30 to 35 minutes

1 small chicken, breast halved,
   then cut into 10 pieces
   and skinned

Salt and freshly ground pepper
   to taste

3 tablespoons olive oil

1 onion, minced

1 large carrot, sliced

4 cups diced tomato

3 garlic cloves, minced

2½ teaspoons minced fresh
   oregano, or ¾ teaspoon
   dried oregano, crumbled

1 tablespoon minced fresh thyme,
   or 1 teaspoon dried thyme

1 tablespoon minced fresh rosemary
   leaves, or 1 teaspoon dried
   rosemary, crumbled

2 bay leaves, or to taste

1 cup dry red wine

2 cups water

1 Knorr chicken bouillon cube,
   crumbled

4 sun-dried tomatoes, chopped

⅛ to ¼ teaspoon dried red pepper
   (optional)

15 green olives

3 tablespoons minced fresh
   parsley leaves

1. Rinse the chicken, pat it dry, and season with salt and pepper. In a large casserole set over moderately high heat, warm 2 tablespoons of the oil until hot. Add the chicken and cook it until no longer pink on all sides. Transfer to a plate.

2. Heat the remaining oil in the casserole over moderate heat until hot. Add the onion, carrot, and salt and pepper to taste, and cook, stirring occasionally, for 3 minutes, or until softened. Add the tomato, garlic, oregano, thyme, rosemary, and bay leaves, and cook the mixture, stirring occasionally, for 5 minutes more. Return the chicken to the casserole, add the wine, and reduce it over moderately high heat for 1 minute. Add the water, bouillon cube, sun-dried tomatoes, dried red pepper, if desired, and more salt to taste, bring to a boil, and simmer, stirring occasionally, for 15 minutes more, or until chicken is tender. Add olives and cook 5 minutes more.

3. Transfer chicken to a serving plate and reduce sauce over moderately high heat until lightly thickened. Discard bay leaves, spoon sauce over chicken, and sprinkle with parsley.

Serves 6.

(Per serving) Calories: 467; Protein: 36g; Fat: 16g; Carbohydrates: 95g; Cholesterol: 93mg; Sodium: 10mg.

Food always means something beyond the fact of what we put into our mouths. Food, I found, is about loving and living and dying.

—*Paul Schmidt*

MARIA'S MEAT PIE

Prep Time: 20 minutes
Cook Time: 20 minutes

I frequent a trattoria in my neighborhood in Milan, Latteria San Marco, which is run by a sweet couple named Arturo & Maria. Because it is so small, patrons end up sharing tables with people they don't know, and this adds to the homey atmosphere. Soon the regulars become friends anyway.

2 tablespoons olive oil, plus
    additional for drizzling
    over the pie
1 onion, minced
1 pound zucchini, trimmed
    and sliced thin
1/2 teaspoon Herbes de Provence
Salt and freshly ground black
    pepper to taste
3/4 pound ground veal
1 large egg, beaten lightly
5 tablespoons minced
    fresh parsley

2 cloves garlic,
    finely minced
1 1/2 teaspoons each minced
    fresh thyme and rosemary
    leaves, or 1/2 teaspoon each
    dried mint and rosemary,
    crumbled
1/2 teaspoon Cavender's Greek
    seasoning, if available
1/2 cup dried or fresh
    bread crumbs
1/2 cup freshly grated Parmesan,
    or to taste

1. Preheat oven to 350°F.

2. In a nonstick skillet set over moderately high heat, warm the oil until it is hot, add the onion and cook it, stirring occasionally, for 3 minutes. Add the zucchini, Herbes de Provence, salt, and pepper, and cook, stirring occasionally, for 3 to 5 minutes more, or until lightly golden. Let cool.

3. In a bowl combine the veal, egg, 3 tablespoons of the parsley, the garlic, herbs, Cavender's Greek seasoning, and salt and pepper to taste.

4. In a 9-inch greased pie pan sprinkle 2 to 3 tablespoons of the bread crumbs, or enough to coat the bottom of the pan evenly. Add half of the zucchini mixture to the pan, arranging it in an even layer, top with the meat and finally cover with the remaining zucchini.

5. In a bowl combine the remaining parsley, bread crumbs, and the Parmesan and sprinkle the mixture over the top of the pie. Drizzle with a little oil.

6. Bake the pie in the oven for 20 minutes, or until cooked through and golden. Let cool slightly before serving. It can be served warm or at room temperature.

Serves 6.

(Per serving) Calories: 229; Protein: 17g; Fat: 12g;
Carbohydrates: 13g; Cholesterol: 82mg; Sodium: 274mg.

SCALLOPINE
ALLA PIZZIOLA

Prep Time: 10 minutes
Cook Time: 10 minutes

4 veal cutlets (about 1 pound)

Flour for dredging the veal

Salt and freshly ground
    black pepper

3 tablespoons olive oil

1 tablespoon minced fresh rosemary,
    or 1 teaspoon dried rosemary,
    crumbled

1½ teaspoons minced fresh oregano,
    or ½ teaspoon dried oregano,
    crumbled

3 garlic cloves, peeled and smashed

8 plum tomatoes, cored and quartered

⅛ to ¼ teaspoon dried red pepper
    flakes

2 tablespoons minced fresh basil

1. Lightly dredge the veal in the flour, shaking off the excess, and season
with salt and pepper to taste.

2. In a large nonstick skillet set over moderately high heat, warm the oil
until it is hot, add the herbs and garlic, and cook, stirring, until garlic is
golden brown. Push the garlic to the side of the pan and add the veal. Cook
veal for 1 minute on each side or until golden brown and transfer to platter.
Add tomatoes and salt and red pepper flakes to taste to the pan and cook,
stirring, for 3 minutes, or until tomatoes are softened and skin loosened.

3. Return veal to pan and simmer until just heated through. Stir in basil
and transfer to serving plates. Serve with a crisp salad.

Serves 4.

(Per serving) Calories: 266; Protein: 24g; Fat: 15g;
Carbohydrates: 9g; Cholesterol: 95mg; Sodium: 110mg.

> Pure men like pure food which gives good health, balanced mentality, sustaining strength . . . Pure food that promotes the knowledge of God.
>
> —*Bhagavad Gita*

Most of my family is scattered within two states of southern India— Tamil Nadu and Kerala. These two bordering states have similar cuisines and many of the dishes made with coconut are indicative of this region. As a girl, I remember many visits to my grandmother's coconut farm in Tanjore where the gardener would humor our capricious wishes by letting us pick out the exact coconut to chop down for each of us to sip in the veranda as we cooled off from the day's play. I don't know how that poor man clung as long as he did to the tree trunk as we fought over which coconut was the biggest. Years later, when I started to eat meat, I went back to try some of the local nonvegetarian specialties. As children, we were forbidden to eat non-Brahmin foods (the Brahmin diet is lacto-vegetarian), and I soon found out there was a whole other side to Tamilian gastronomy.

My recipe for coconut chicken is a re-creation of what I tasted at a truck stop on a long cross-country drive with my three uncles. The trip was actually only three hundred miles, but it seemed much longer as it consisted mostly of narrow streets that went through various South Indian village towns. We shared the road with everything from rickshaws, scooters, and vegetable carts moving at a snail's pace, to goats in herds and the occasional cow. We were on our way to Trichy from Madras and somewhere near Mathurai, our old black Ambassador got a flat tire. We stopped for a late supper while waiting for the car to be repaired at the only place that was open at that hour of the night. My seven-year-old body was tired from the bumpy road, the long hours in the car, and I was badly in need of a shower. I resented my mother dragging me across India to show me to all her relatives. Every time we made a return trip to India my mother was adamant about visiting all her relatives, as well as the old neighbors of her relatives and the in-laws of her relatives. Needless to say, I had quickly become a very irritable girl. Yet all my weariness started to melt away when the waiter, wearing nothing more than an undershirt and veshti (a saronglike fabric tied as a towel around the waist), brought us a chipped enamel bowl of rice covered with chicken stewed in coconut.

INDIA

COCONUT CHICKEN

Prep Time: *15 to 20 minutes*
Cook Time: *30 minutes*

1 onion, coarsely chopped

3 cloves garlic, chopped

1 tablespoon minced fresh gingerroot

1 large jalapeño chili, stemmed
and halved, or to taste (Chilies
vary considerably in heat so go
carefully.)

Grated zest of 1 lemon, about 1
tablespoon

1/4 cup water

2 tablespoons vegetable oil

One 3- to 3 1/2-pound chicken, cut into
small serving pieces, skin removed

1 cup sliced carrots

Salt to taste

1 1/2 teaspoons Hot Madras Sambar
Curry Powder*

One 14-ounce can unsweetened
"light" coconut milk

Fresh lemon juice to taste

1/2 to 1 cup loosely packed chopped
fresh cilantro leaves

1. In a blender combine the onion, garlic, gingerroot, chili, lemon zest, and water and blend until puréed.

2. In a casserole set over moderate heat, warm the oil until it is hot. Add the paste and cook it, stirring, for 3 minutes. Add the chicken, carrots, and salt to taste, and cook, turning the chicken until lightly colored on both sides, for about 10 minutes. Add the curry powder and cook, stirring and turning, for 5 minutes. Add the coconut milk and simmer, stirring occasionally, for about 10 minutes, or until chicken is cooked through. Stir in the lemon juice to taste and the cilantro. Serve with rice.

Serves 4.

Variation: Other vegetables, such as canned baby corn, sliced zucchini, and cut green beans can be added to complete the dish, if desired.

*Hot Madras curry powder is available at specialty food shops.

(Per serving) Calories: 354; Protein: 53g; Fat: 10g;
Carbohydrates: 13g; Cholesterol: 127mg; Sodium: 178mg.

RANI RICE PILAF

Prep Time: *5 minutes*
Cook Time: *25 to 30 minutes*

2 tablespoons vegetable oil

1 onion, minced

2 cloves garlic, minced

1 teaspoon minced gingerroot

1 cinnamon stick

5 green cardamom pods

2½ cups Basmati
   or other long-grain rice

4½ cups water

Salt to taste

½ to 1 cup golden raisins,
   if desired

In a saucepan set over moderate heat, warm the oil until it is hot, add the onion and garlic, and cook, stirring, until golden. Add the gingerroot, cinnamon stick, and cardamom, and cook, stirring, 1 minute. Add the rice and cook, stirring, until rice is coated with oil. Add the water and salt, bring to a boil, and simmer, covered, 20 minutes. Stir in raisins and let stand, covered, 5 minutes. Remove cinnamon stick before serving.

Makes about 8 cups.

(Per serving) Calories: 525; Protein: 11g; Fat: 9g; Carbohydrates: 100g; Cholesterol: 0mg; Sodium: 88mg.

NIMBU RICE

RICE WITH INDIAN SPICES, CASHEWS, AND CHILIES

Prep Time: 5 minutes
Cook Time: 10 to 12 minutes

3 tablespoons vegetable oil

3 tablespoons gram lentils*

1/2 teaspoon asafetida powder†

1 teaspoon turmeric

2 to 4 hot green chilies, such as
   jalapeño, sliced

1 1/2 teaspoons black mustard
   seeds

2/3 cup raw cashew nuts

8 cups cold cooked rice

Juice of 1 lemon, or to taste

Salt to taste

In a casserole set over moderate heat, warm the oil, add the lentils, asafetida powder, turmeric, and chilies and cook, stirring, until sizzling. Add the mustard seeds and cashew nuts, and cook, stirring, for 5 minutes. Add the rice, lemon juice, and salt to taste and cook, stirring occasionally, until heated through.

Serves 6 to 8.

*Gram lentils are available at specialty food shops.
†Asafetida powder is available at specialty food shops.

**(Per serving) Calories: 632; Protein: 13g; Fat: 8g;
Carbohydrates: 123g; Cholesterol: 0mg; Sodium: 9mg.**

SOUTH INDIAN
SQUASH SOUP

Prep Time: *5 minutes*
Cook Time: *20 minutes*

8 large yellow squash, sliced thick

2 large tomatoes, quartered

Salt to taste

1 Knorr vegetable bouillon cube

1 tablespoon coconut powder, or
   grated unsweetened coconut

2 teaspoons vegetable oil

2 tablespoons slivered almonds

2 teaspoons cumin seeds

6 dried red chilies, or to taste

1½ teaspoons black mustard seeds

10 curry leaves*

1. In a large saucepan or casserole, combine the squash and tomatoes. Add enough water to just cover, salt to taste, and bouillon cube, bring liquid to a boil, and add the coconut powder. Simmer for 10 minutes, stirring occasionally, or until squash is tender.

2. In a blender or food processor purée the soup in batches and return it to the pan.

3. In a small skillet set over moderate heat, warm the oil until hot. Add the almonds and cook, stirring, 30 seconds. Add the cumin seeds, red chilies, black mustard seeds, and curry leaves, and cook, stirring, until mustard seeds begin to pop. Transfer mixture to soup, add salt to taste, and simmer until heated through.

Serves 4.

*Curry leaves are available at specialty food shops.

(**Per serving**) **Calories: 162; Protein: 7g; Fat: 5g;
Carbohydrates: 26g; Cholesterol: 0mg; Sodium: 377mg.**

TANDOORI CHICKEN SALAD

Prep Time: 25 minutes

Cook Time: 10 minutes

For the yogurt marinade:

1 cup plain nonfat yogurt

2 teaspoons Garam Masala powder*

1 teaspoon ground ginger

1 teaspoon minced garlic

1 teaspoon ground turmeric

1 teaspoon salt

1 jalapeño chili, stemmed, seeded,
  and finely minced (optional)

4 (1½ pounds) skinless, boneless chicken
  breast halves, gently flattened and cut
  into strips

For the salad:

3 cups shredded iceberg lettuce
  (1 small head)

3 cups shredded red cabbage
  (1 small head)

3 cups diced plum tomatoes
  (about 6 large)

1 cup sliced radishes (1 bunch)

2 cups sliced cucumber (1 large)

1 small bunch scallions, minced

1 cup loosely packed cilantro leaves,
  finely chopped

1½ cups diced jicama

1 tablespoon vegetable oil

Juice of 2 to 3 small lemons, or to taste

Salt and freshly ground black pepper to
  taste

1. **Make the marinade:** In a bowl combine all ingredients. Arrange chicken in a shallow dish, add the marinade, and stir to coat with the marinade. Cover and chill while preparing the vegetables.

2. **Make the salad:** In a large salad bowl combine all salad ingredients.

3. In a nonstick skillet set over moderately high heat, warm the oil until it is hot. Add the chicken and marinade and cook, stirring, until the chicken is no longer pink. (Yogurt will separate.) Let simmer just until cooked.

4. Transfer chicken together with pan juices to salad bowl and toss to combine. Add lemon juice and salt and pepper to taste.

Serves 6.   *Garam Masala is available at specialty food shops.

(Per serving) Calories: 469; Protein: 69g; Fat: 6g;
Carbohydrates: 31g; Cholesterol: 160mg; Sodium: 600mg.

When I was a child traveling with my relatives one of my great adventures was eating from street vendors, a luxury only locals can afford, as street fare can be risky, but even as a toddler I was already fearless. I reveled, wide-eyed, in the commotion. I love the smell of crackling cumin in hot oil, the clanging of greasy ladles, and the chopping of chilies so hot even the grown man doing it would have fear in his eyes. I could stand more piquant dishes than most of the elders accompanying me. We often ate from disposable bowls made from dry lily leaves. A piece of bread was the only cutlery used, and this soon led to a sizzling dish called Pav Bhadji. It is a fiery dish of puréed vegetables and lentils, made in a gigantic wok, drenched in ghee or butter. This black iron altar usually sits on an oil drum filled with coals, wood, paper, and twigs burning at great heat. The mixture is turned and stirred by a skillful cook at a rapid pace to ensure even temperatures. The piping hot concoction is then spooned into one of the leaf bowls and served with a piece of soft bread. There was never enough bread for sopping up all the Bhadji, so I always used my fingers. It gave me an excuse to lick my fingers afterward, and if I could get away with it, lick the bowl slyly as well. Of course, having grown up and tried to curtail my unhealthier impulses, I had to forget about such greasy delights. But, the tastes invoked by Pav Bhadji are similar to chick-pea dishes from North India called chole or chana. Chole is served with fried crêpes called puris, which I have omitted, but I eat it over plain rice and still manage to feel the heat of that great oil drum on my face.

CHOLE

CHICK-PEA CURRY

Prep Time: *10 minutes*
Cook Time: *25 to 30 minutes*

2 onions, quartered

1 green bell pepper, cored, seeded, and chopped

6 large firm, ripe tomatoes

2 tablespoons chopped gingerroot

2 tablespoons vegetable oil

1 tablespoon Garam Masala*

1/2 teaspoon red chili powder, or to taste

Salt to taste

Two 15-ounce cans chick-peas or garbanzo beans, drained and rinsed

2 to 3 tablespoons fresh lemon juice, or to taste

1 to 2 tablespoons minced fresh cilantro, or to taste

1. In a blender or food processor purée the onions, green pepper, tomatoes, and gingerroot.

2. In a saucepan set over moderate heat, warm the oil until hot. Add the purée and cook, stirring occasionally, for 20 minutes. Add the Garam Masala and chili powder and cook, stirring occasionally, for 5 minutes. Add the salt and chick-peas and cook, stirring, until heated through. Stir in the lemon juice and cilantro. Serve the curry over rice or with warmed tortillas.

Serves 4 to 6.

*Garam Masala is available at specialty food shops.

(Per serving) Calories: 279; Protein: 9g; Fat: 7g;
Carbohydrates: 47g; Cholesterol: 0mg; Sodium: 445mg.

RAJMA

VEGETARIAN CHILI

Originally from North India, this dish could be called vegetarian chili. You may serve it in a bowl over rice or with warmed tortillas like the Chole. In North India, flat breads such as nan or chapati are eaten with curries. In South India, rice is more common as an accompaniment, although we also eat crêpes made of rice flour, called dosai.

Prep Time: 10 minutes
Cook Time: 25 minutes

2 tablespoons vegetable oil

1 cup minced onions

1 green bell pepper, diced

2 cloves garlic, minced

4 firm, ripe tomatoes,
    cut into 1-inch pieces

2 teaspoons minced gingerroot,
    or 1 teaspoon ground ginger

1 teaspoon cumin seeds

1 teaspoon Garam Masala*

1/2 teaspoon lemon pepper

1/4 teaspoon dried red pepper
    flakes, or to taste (optional)

2 cups drained canned kidney
    beans (19-ounce can)

Salt and freshly ground pepper
    to taste

Juice of 1/2 lemon, or to taste

3 tablespoons minced fresh cilantro

*Garam Masala is available at specialty food shops.

In a large saucepan set over moderate heat, warm the oil until hot, add the onions and pepper, and cook, stirring occasionally, for 5 minutes. Add the garlic, tomatoes, gingerroot, cumin seeds, Garam Masala, lemon pepper, and dried red pepper flakes, if desired, and simmer the mixture, stirring occasionally, for 10 minutes. Add the beans and salt and pepper to taste, and cook, stirring occasionally, for 5 minutes more. Stir in the lemon juice and cilantro.

Serves 4.

(Per serving) Calories: 224; Protein: 9g; Fat: 8g;
Carbohydrates: 32g; Cholesterol: 0mg; Sodium: 571mg.

'Tis an ill cook that cannot lick his own fingers.

—William Shakespeare

HALIBUT WITH CABBAGE

Prep Time: 20 minutes

Cook Time: 16 to 20 minutes

2 tablespoons vegetable oil

1½ teaspoons black mustard
   seeds

1 teaspoon cumin seeds

6 dried red chilies, or to taste

1 onion, sliced

1 tablespoon minced
   gingerroot

4 cups chopped green cabbage

1 zucchini, cut into
   ¼-inch-thick slices

Salt to taste

1 pound halibut, cut into
   1½-inch pieces

One 14-ounce can "light"
   unsweetened coconut milk

½ cup minced fresh cilantro

Lemon juice to taste

1. In a casserole set over moderate heat, warm the oil until hot, add the mustard seeds, cumin seeds, and chilies, and cook, stirring, 1 minute, or until seeds begin to pop. Add the onion and cook, stirring, 5 minutes. Add the gingerroot, cabbage, zucchini, and salt to taste, and cook, stirring occasionally, for 5 minutes.

2. Add the halibut, season with salt and cook, gently stirring, 1 to 2 minutes, or until fish is lightly colored. Add the coconut milk, bring to a simmer and cook, covered, stirring occasionally, for 3 to 4 minutes more, or until fish is just cooked. Add the cilantro and season with the lemon juice to taste.

Serves 4.

(Per serving) Calories: 303; Protein: 30g; Fat: 11g;
Carbohydrates: 26g; Cholesterol: 36mg; Sodium: 162mg.

**Sharing food with another human being is an
intimate act that should not be indulged in lightly.**

—*M.F.K. Fisher*

CHIDAMBARAM CHICKEN

Prep Time: *10 minutes*

Cook Time: *12 to 15 minutes*

2 whole skinless, boneless chicken
    breasts, halved and cut into
    1-inch pieces
Salt and freshly ground pepper to taste
2 tablespoons vegetable oil
2 onions, chopped
2 red bell peppers, chopped

2 large cloves garlic, minced
1 to 2 teaspoons Garam Masala*
1/8 to 1/4 teaspoon dried red pepper
    flakes, or to taste (optional)
1 cup nonfat plain yogurt
1/2 cup minced fresh mint,
    or to taste

In a large nonstick skillet set over moderate heat, cook the chicken, seasoned with salt and pepper, in the oil, stirring, until no longer pink. With a slotted spoon transfer the chicken to a plate. Add the onions, peppers, and garlic to the pan, and cook, stirring occasionally, for 5 minutes. Return the chicken to the pan, add the Garam Masala and red pepper, if desired, and cook, stirring, for 3 minutes. Add the yogurt and additional salt to taste, and simmer just until chicken is cooked. Stir in the mint and correct seasoning.

Serves 4.

*Garam Masala is available at specialty food shops.

**(Per serving) Calories: 228; Protein: 23g; Fat: 8g;
Carbohydrates: 14g; Cholesterol: 49mg; Sodium: 168mg.**

TURAN'S TUNA CURRY

Prep Time: 10 minutes

Cook Time: 12 to 15 minutes

2 tablespoons vegetable oil

½ onion, minced

½ green bell pepper, minced

2 garlic cloves, minced

1 teaspoon minced gingerroot

½ teaspoon hot Madras curry powder*

Three 6-ounce cans tuna packed in
   spring water, drained

1 to 2 green serrano or jalapeño
   chilies, stemmed, seeded, and
   minced, or to taste

Salt to taste

Juice of ½ lemon or lime

⅓ to ½ cup chopped fresh cilantro,
   or to taste

1. In a skillet set over moderate heat, warm the oil until it is hot. Add the onion and pepper, and cook, stirring, for 5 minutes, or until softened. Add the garlic, gingerroot, and curry powder, and cook, stirring, for 2 minutes.

2. Add the tuna, chilies, and salt and cook, stirring, until heated through. Season with lemon or lime juice and toss with cilantro. Serve with rice or as a filling for flour tortillas.

Serves 4.

*Hot Madras curry powder is available at specialty food shops.

(Per serving) Calories: 234; Protein: 33g; Fat: 8g;
Carbohydrates: 5g; Cholesterol: 38mg; Sodium: 505mg.

CHICKEN WITH MANGO CHUTNEY

Making decent mango chutney at home in America is a tricky business. It is difficult to find green mangoes. In the summer months they are at good Asian markets. If one is ambitious, a simple mango chutney can be made by puréeing the meat of a green mango in a blender with two green chilis and salt to taste, but I like Patak's the best because it's not too sweet. This chutney is great on sandwiches as well.

> Prep Time: *30 minutes, including marinating*
> Cook Time: *1 1/4 hours*

6 whole chicken legs (drumsticks and thighs), skinned, rinsed, and patted dry

3 tablespoons olive oil

1 tablespoon each minced fresh thyme, rosemary, and tarragon leaves, or 1 teaspoon each dried thyme, rosemary, and tarragon, crumbled

1 to 2 teaspoons lemon pepper seasoning, or to taste

6 tablespoons Patak's Hot Mango Chutney*

1 tablespoon Dijon mustard

Salad greens as an accompaniment

1. In a shallow dish, arrange the chicken in one layer.

2. In a bowl whisk together the oil, herbs, and lemon pepper seasoning. Pour mixture over chicken, coating both sides, and let marinate, covered and chilled, for 20 minutes.

3. Preheat the oven to 350°F.

4. Transfer the chicken to a shallow baking pan along with the marinade, coat with the chutney and mustard and cover with foil.

5. Bake the chicken in the oven for 1 to 1¼ hours, basting frequently, or until tender. Uncover during last 15 minutes of cooking. Run under pre-heated broiler until lightly colored before serving, if desired.

6. Transfer chicken legs to a serving platter and surround them with the salad greens.

Serves 6.   *Patak's Hot Mango Chutney is available at specialty food shops.

(Per serving) Calories: 274; Protein: 28g; Fat: 12g; Carbohydrates: 10g; Cholesterol: 113mg; Sodium: 214mg.

KEEMA

INDIAN SPICED GROUND VEAL AND BEEF WITH PEAS

When my mother and I first moved to California, we lived near an Indian couple, Nirmal and Pratima. As my mother worked late in the evening, I often dropped by their house for dinner. It dawns on me now that I might have been a bother, but when I first started eating meat, it was Pratima's keema that I liked best. I suppose the ground beef didn't look very much like meat to me, and the taste was exquisite. Even as a young girl I had an appetite for fiery fare, and Pratima seemed more than happy to oblige by slicing up chilies for me to mix into my keema.

Prep Time: *8 minutes*

Cook Time: *20 to 25 minutes*

2 tablespoons vegetable oil
1 onion, minced
8 ounces ground veal
8 ounces ground lean beef
Salt and freshly ground pepper to taste
2 large cloves garlic, minced
2 firm, ripe tomatoes, diced
1 tablespoon minced gingerroot, or 1 teaspoon ground ginger

1 teaspoon Garam Masala*
1 teaspoon minced fresh hot green chilies, or to taste
3 cups frozen peas
Juice of one lemon, or to taste
2 to 3 tablespoons minced fresh cilantro, or to taste
Indian flatbreads (rotis) or tortillas as an accompaniment

1. In a nonstick skillet set over moderately high heat, warm the oil until hot. Add the onion and cook, stirring occasionally, 5 minutes. Add the veal, beef, and salt and pepper to taste, and cook, stirring, until no longer pink.

2. Add the garlic, tomatoes, gingerroot, Garam Masala, and chilies, and cook, stirring, for 5 minutes. Add the peas and continue to cook over moderate heat, stirring occasionally, for 10 minutes more, or until flavors blend.

3. Stir in the lemon juice and cilantro and correct seasoning, adding more salt if necessary. Either transfer to a bowl and serve with warm rotis or tortillas or spoon Keema down center of bread and roll up like a burrito.

Serves 4 to 6.   *Garam Masala is available at specialty food shops.

(Per serving) Calories: 179; Protein: 14g; Fat: 8g; Carbohydrates: 11g; Cholesterol: 43mg; Sodium: 139mg.

> My kitchen is a mystical place, a kind of
> temple for me. It is a place where the
> surfaces seem to have significance, where the
> sounds and odors carry meaning that transfers
> from the past and bridges to the future.
>
> —*Pearl Bailey*

Bali is one of my favorite places in the world. The Balinese, unlike the rest of Indonesians, are Hindus, so I feel very much at home. The best thing about Bali is, of course, the food. A healthy assortment of pan-Asian food is available and choices from Indian to Japanese dishes are often found in the same restaurant. My first time there, on vacation, I ate so well, that my taste buds were in a constant state of bliss the whole trip.

Perhaps the only drawback to going to Bali is the notoriously long flight. I flew back to Milan, exhausted, and after two days I boarded another plane for Los Angeles to surprise my mother on her fiftieth birthday. I had planned to spend ten days with her. Shortly after I had gained the stamina to unpack (the jet lag was getting to me) I received a call from Dawn, my booker in Paris. She informed me that a French catalogue wanted me to fly back to Bali the next day for a shoot. So with my mother feeling disappointed and me not feeling much of anything but exhaustion, I boarded the plane at L.A. International back to Denpasar.

That whole trip was arduous, and had it been anywhere else I wouldn't have survived. I did, however, impress the client by knowing all the great places to eat, and even suggested a few locations. After spending a whole month in Bali, my palate became a culinary detective. I have been able to reconstruct several of my favorite foods, and they still remind me of my time in Bali.

MI GORENG

Prep Time: 15 minutes
Cook Time: 20 minutes

½ pound linguine

Salt

2 tablespoons vegetable oil

1 cup minced onions

2 teaspoons minced gingerroot,
    or 1 teaspoon ground ginger

2 cloves garlic, minced

3 cups broccoli florets

2 carrots, diced

2 celery stalks, diced

1 teaspoon Chinese five-spice powder

1 teaspoon chili paste, or to taste*

2 tablespoons soy sauce, or to taste

1 to 2 tablespoons Oriental sesame oil

1 tablespoon mango chutney

1. In a large pot of boiling salted water cook the linguine until it is *al dente* and drain, reserving ½ cup of pasta cooking liquid.

2. Meanwhile, prepare the vegetables: In a large nonstick skillet set over moderately high heat, warm the oil until hot, add the onions, gingerroot, and garlic, and cook, stirring occasionally, for 3 minutes. Add the broccoli, carrots, celery, and salt to taste and cook, stirring, for 5 minutes more. Add the five-spice powder, chili paste, soy sauce, and ½ cup of pasta cooking liquid, and cook, stirring occasionally, until vegetables are crisp-tender. Stir in the sesame oil and chutney. Add the drained pasta and stir to combine.

Serves 4.

*Chili paste is available at specialty food shops.

(Per serving) Calories: 416; Protein: 12g; Fat: 15g;
Carbohydrates: 60g; Cholesterol: 0mg; Sodium: 568mg.

RAMEN STIR-FRY

NOODLE, VEGETABLE, AND CHICKEN STIR-FRY

Anyone who went to college in the United States knows the many uses of Oodles of Noodles or Top Ramen instant noodles. Not only are they inexpensive, but they come in handy under all sorts of time constraints. This recipe has saved me from countless days of starvation. And it doesn't take that long either. You can slice up the vegetables ahead of time and vary the ingredients to your taste.

Prep Time: 20 minutes

Cook Time: 12 to 15 minutes

Two 3-ounce packages Ramen noodles,
   such as chicken or mushroom
2 tablespoons vegetable oil
1 teaspoon minced gingerroot
2 teaspoons minced garlic
1 small onion, minced
2 carrots, thinly sliced
3 celery stalks, thickly sliced
8 ounces shiitake mushrooms, wiped

cleaned, trimmed and sliced
1 boneless and skinless chicken breast
   (1 pound), cut into 1-inch pieces
1½ cups broccoli florets
2 to 3 tablespoons Szechuan stir-fry
   sauce, or to taste
½ to 1 teaspoon chili paste,
   or to taste*
1 tablespoon minced fresh cilantro

1. Following directions on package, cook the noodles and drain, reserving ½ cup cooking liquid.

2. Meanwhile, prepare the stir-fry: In a wok or large skillet set over moderately high heat, warm the oil until it is hot, add the gingerroot and garlic and stir-fry 30 seconds, or until fragrant. Add the onion, carrots, and celery, and stir-fry 2 minutes. Add the mushrooms and stir-fry 3 minutes more. Add the chicken and broccoli, and stir-fry until chicken is no longer pink. Add the seasonings from the Ramen packages along with the Szechuan sauce, and stir-fry 1 minute. Add the reserved 1/2 cup cooking liquid and let simmer, stirring occasionally, until chicken is thoroughly cooked. Add the noodles to the pan and cook, stirring, just until heated through. Season with the chili paste and cilantro.

Serves 4.   *Chili paste is available at specialty food shops.

(**Per serving) Calories:** 582; **Protein:** 38g; **Fat:** 13g;
Carbohydrates: 83g; **Cholesterol:** 110mg; **Sodium:** 142mg.

ORIENTAL SHRIMP SALAD

Prep Time: 30 minutes

Cook Time: 3 to 4 minutes

For the shrimp paste:

1 cup loosely packed mint leaves

1 small onion, coarsely chopped

1 tablespoon minced gingerroot

12 black peppercorns, coarsely crushed

1 teaspoon ground cumin

1 teaspoon tamarind paste*

1/2 teaspoon sugar

1/3 cup water

Salt to taste

2 pounds large shrimp, shelled and
  deveined

For the vegetables:

4 cups shredded iceberg lettuce

3 cups grated carrots

2 cups diced celery

2 cups shredded red cabbage

5 scallions, minced

1 cup loosely packed cilantro leaves,
  minced (after measuring)

For the dressing:

3 tablespoons fresh lime or lemon juice

2 tablespoons Oriental sesame oil

2 tablespoons soy sauce

1 tablespoon rice wine vinegar

3 dashes Oriental hot chili oil, or to taste

Salt to taste

Spray-on vegetable oil

3 tablespoons toasted sesame seeds
  for garnish

ASIA

◆

80

1. **Make the paste:** In a blender combine the first nine ingredients and blend until puréed.

2. In a bowl toss the shrimp with the paste and let marinate while preparing the vegetables.

3. **Make the salad:** In a large salad bowl combine the six salad vegetables.

4. **Make the dressing:** In a bowl whisk together the six salad dressing ingredients.

5. Spray a large skillet set over moderately high heat with some vegetable oil and heat until hot. Add the shrimp and cook, turning, for 3 to 4 minutes, or until just cooked. Add the shrimp to the salad bowl, drizzle with dressing to taste, and toss. Divide among serving dishes and sprinkle with the sesame seeds.

Serves 6 generously.   *Tamarind paste is available at specialty food shops.

(Per serving) Calories: 303; Protein: 36g; Fat: 8g;
Carbohydrates: 22g; Cholesterol: 230mg; Sodium: 629mg.

THAI CHICKEN STEW

Outside it's wet and gray, the kind of day that makes one want to stay inside. The best recipe on days like this is a hot pot of stew, something savory to shake the dullness of the day from overtaking you with numbness. One dish guaranteed to help is a Thai chicken stew. Take your time. Concentrate on the joys of the voyage rather than arriving at the destination. Enjoy the activity.

Prep Time: 20 minutes
Cook Time: 45 minutes

1½ pounds chicken legs, separated
   into drumsticks and thighs,
   skin removed
Salt to taste
2 tablespoons vegetable oil
1 cup minced onion
5 cloves garlic, peeled
1 tablespoon grated gingerroot
1 cup sliced carrots
1 cup 1-inch pieces red bell pepper
1 cup sliced mushrooms
1 to 2 teaspoons red curry paste*,
   or to taste
Two 14-ounce cans "light"
   unsweetened coconut milk

½ teaspoon galanga root powder†
½ teaspoon dried lemongrass flakes‡
1 teaspoon ground cumin
1 bay leaf
1 cup broccoli florets
½ cup canned bamboo shoots,
   drained
½ cup canned water chestnuts,
   drained
8 ears canned baby corn, drained
Fresh lemon juice to taste
¼ cup minced fresh cilantro
¼ cup minced fresh mint

*Red curry paste is available in specialty food shops.
†Galanga root powder is available at specialty food shops.
‡Lemongrass flakes are available at specialty food shops.

1. Pat the chicken dry and season with salt.

2. In a casserole set over moderately high heat, warm the oil until it is hot, add the chicken and cook it, turning, until no longer pink. Transfer chicken to a plate.

3. Add the onion to the casserole and cook it, stirring occasionally, for 3 minutes. Add the garlic and gingerroot and cook, stirring, 1 minute. Add the carrots, bell pepper, mushrooms, and salt to taste, and cook the mixture, stirring occasionally, for 5 minutes more.

4. Return the chicken to the pan, add the curry paste and cook the mixture, turning and stirring, 1 minute. Add the coconut milk, galanga root powder, lemongrass flakes, cumin, and bay leaf. Bring mixture to a boil, and simmer, stirring occasionally, for 20 minutes.

5. Add the broccoli, bamboo shoots, water chestnuts, corn, and salt to taste, and simmer the mixture, stirring occasionally, for 10 minutes, or until chicken is cooked through. Discard bay leaf. Before serving, stir in the lemon juice, cilantro, and mint.

Serves 4.

(Per serving) Calories: 344; Protein: 30g; Fat: 15g; Carbohydrates: 27g; Cholesterol: 66mg; Sodium: 338mg.

PAN-ASIAN FRIED RICE

Prep Time: *40 minutes*

Cook Time: *15 to 20 minutes*

For the rice:

3 cups water

1 Knorr chicken bouillon cube

3 small bay leaves

1 tablespoon Oriental sesame oil

Salt to taste

1½ cups Uncle Ben's converted rice

For the egg sheets:

2 large eggs

2 egg whites

Salt to taste

1 tablespoon oil

3 tablespoons vegetable oil

4 cloves garlic, minced

1 tablespoon minced gingerroot

1 onion, chopped

1 green bell pepper,
   cut into 1-inch pieces

2 carrots, thinly sliced

½ pound shiitake mushrooms, wiped
   clean, trimmed and sliced

Salt to taste

4 stalks celery, thickly sliced

3 cups coarsely chopped green cabbage

1 tablespoon Garam Masala*

¼ to ⅓ cup Szechuan stir-fry sauce,
   or to taste

One 8-ounce can bamboo shoots,
   drained

One 8-ounce can water chestnuts,
   drained

2 to 3 teaspoons chili paste,
   or to taste†

2 to 3 teaspoons Oriental sesame oil,
   or to taste

½ cup minced fresh cilantro,
   or to taste

1. **Make the rice:** In a saucepan set over moderately high heat bring the water to a boil, add the bouillon cube, bay leaves, sesame oil, and salt to taste, and stir to dissolve bouillon. Add the rice, bring back to the boil, stirring, and simmer, covered, for 20 minutes. Let stand for 5 minutes. Transfer rice to a bowl and fluff with a fork. Discard bay leaves.

2. **Make the egg sheets:** In a bowl whisk together the whole eggs, egg whites, and salt. In a large non-stick skillet set over moderate heat, warm

*Garam Masala is available at specialty food shops.

†Chili paste is available at specialty food shops.

the oil until it is hot, add the egg mixture, lifting and tilting the pan to coat the bottom evenly with the egg, and let it cook until set on the underside. Turn and let cook until eggs are completely set. Transfer to a plate and let cool. Cut into shreds.

3. In a wok or casserole set over moderately high heat, warm the oil until it is hot. Add the garlic and gingerroot and stir-fry for 1 minute, or until fragrant. Add the onion, green pepper, carrots, mushrooms, and salt and stir-fry 5 minutes. Add the celery and cabbage and stir-fry 3 minutes more. Add the Garam Masala and Szechuan sauce, and stir-fry 2 minutes. Add the bamboo shoots, water chestnuts and ½ cup water and let cook, stirring, 3 to 5 minutes, or until vegetables are crisp-tender. Add the rice and egg sheets, and stir-fry until rice is heated through. Season with the chili paste, sesame oil, and cilantro. Adjust seasonings. Transfer mixture to a large serving dish.

Serves 6 generously.

(Per serving) Calories: 498; Protein: 14g; Fat: 15g; Carbohydrates: 83g; Cholesterol: 60mg; Sodium: 1079mg.

BALI BAKED FISH

Prep Time: *10 minutes*

Cook Time: *20 to 25 minutes*

2 pounds red snapper fillets

Salt and freshly ground pepper to taste

1 onion, quartered

3 garlic cloves, chopped

1 tablespoon chopped gingerroot

1 tablespoon tamarind paste*

1 tablespoon Oriental sesame oil

½ teaspoon ground cumin

2 tablespoons water

Fresh lemon juice to taste

3 tablespoons minced fresh mint,
  or to taste

1. Preheat the oven to 350°F.

2. Pat dry the fish fillets, season with salt and pepper, and arrange in a shallow baking dish.

3. In a blender or food processor combine the onion, garlic, gingerroot, tamarind paste, sesame oil, cumin, salt to taste, and 2 tablespoons water and blend until smooth. Pour mixture over fish, coating both sides.

4. Bake fish, covered with foil, in the oven for 20 to 25 minutes, or until it flakes easily with a fork.

5. Transfer fillets to a serving dish, correct seasoning, adding more salt if necessary, and drizzle with lemon juice. Garnish with mint.

Serves 4 to 6.

*Tamarind paste is available at specialty food shops.

(**Per serving**) **Calories: 191; Protein: 32g; Fat: 4g;
Carbohydrates: 3g; Cholesterol: 5mg; Sodium:100g.**

One cannot think well, love well, sleep well, if one has not dined well.

—*Virginia Woolf*

We were in Marrakesh. It was in the desert outside the city, in an area called the Palmiers. It can get cold quite fast late in the day, and Nadir, the photographer, liked the afternoon light of 4:00 P.M. I was dressed in these exquisitely delicate gowns by Chanel made of lace and chiffon. I spent most of the afternoon in tears from the wind and sand. The photos were beautiful and they remain among my favorites to this day.

When we weren't in the desert we shot in open-air food and spice markets, where I was so distracted during the shoot by the colors and aromas around me. A discovery I made in Morocco was the indispensable usefulness of couscous. It's great to use to thicken soups, as a side dish with meat, or alone just seasoned with Harissa or some other hot sauce.

MOROCCO

CHICKEN TAGINE

This is my version of a classical vegetable and chicken stew that is poured over couscous. I find it is easier to cook the couscous right into the stew to save time washing dishes. If desired, the couscous can be made separately and served on the side of the stew.

Prep Time: 20 to 25 minutes

Cook Time: 25 to 30 minutes

3 tablespoons olive oil

1½ pounds skinless boneless chicken breast, cut into strips, and patted dry

1½ cups sliced onions

1½ cups coarsely chopped (about 1-inch pieces) green bell pepper

1½ cups thickly sliced carrots

1½ cups thickly sliced celery

3 cloves garlic, peeled and left whole

Salt and freshly ground pepper to taste

2 teaspoons ground cumin

½ teaspoon ground coriander

3 bay leaves

2 cups cubed (about 1-inch pieces) firm, ripe plum or other tomatoes

2 cups cauliflower florets

6 cups water

1 Knorr chicken bouillon cube

1 lemon, cut into slices, or to taste

2 cups couscous

⅛ to ¼ teaspoon Harissa paste*

1. In a casserole set over moderately high heat, warm 1 tablespoon of the oil until hot. Add the chicken and cook, stirring, until no longer pink. With a slotted spoon transfer to a plate.

2. Add the remaining oil to the casserole, the onions, pepper, carrots, celery, garlic, salt, pepper, cumin, coriander, and bay leaves, and cook the mixture over moderate heat, covered, stirring occasionally, for 5 minutes. Add the tomatoes and cauliflower and cook, stirring, 3 minutes more. Add the water, bouillon cube, and lemon slices, bring to a boil, and simmer, covered, 5 minutes, or until vegetables are just tender.

3. Return the chicken to the casserole, add the couscous, and cook over moderate heat, stirring, for 2 minutes. Add the Harissa paste and salt to taste, stir to combine and let stand, covered, off the heat 5 minutes. Remove and discard bay leaves before serving.

Serves 6.   *Harissa is available at specialty food shops.

(Per serving) Calories: 484; Protein: 36g; Fat: 9g; Carbohydrates: 62g; Cholesterol: 66mg; Sodium: 326mg.

Couscous Upma

Couscous, Green Beans, and Tomatoes

There is a meal we eat back home at about four or five in the evening called tiffin. Tiffin, a term used to mean any snack food, has its origin in Colonial India and was used by the British and Indians alike to refer to those snack foods that were commonly eaten at tea time. South India has retained the term to this day. In our home we usually had our tea in the late Madras sun and ate South Indian crêpes called dosais or steamed dumplings called idlis that were also made of rice batter. Another dish I remember eating quite often is upma. It is similar to stuffing and eaten alone or with a simple yogurt raita on the side. In America, my mother made upma with Cream of Wheat or even grits and I don't think I knew the difference. So couscous seemed to be the perfect variation to me. Tiffin is usually a lighter meal so this recipe is good for 4 or 5 people with a good hot cup of spiced Indian tea.

Prep Time: 10 minutes
Cook Time: 20 to 25 minutes

2 tablespoons vegetable oil	4 firm, ripe tomatoes,
1 teaspoon black mustard seeds	cut into 1-inch pieces
1 teaspoon cumin seeds	Salt to taste
1 teaspoon minced gingerroot	2 cups water
2 cloves garlic, minced	1 Knorr chicken bouillon cube
1 onion, minced	$1^2/_3$ cups couscous
1 cup chopped green bell pepper	Fresh lemon juice to taste
2 cups green beans	Minced fresh cilantro to taste

1. In a deep nonstick skillet set over moderate heat, warm the oil until it is hot. Add the mustard seeds and cumin seeds, and cook, stirring, 1 minute. Add the gingerroot and garlic, and cook, stirring, 1 minute more.

2. Add the onion and green bell pepper to the seasonings and cook, stirring occasionally, for 5 minutes.

3. Add the green beans, tomatoes, and salt, and cook, stirring occasionally, for 5 minutes more.

4. Add the water, bouillon cube, and salt to taste, bring to a boil, stirring, and add couscous. Simmer, stirring occasionally, for 5 to 10 minutes, or until liquid is just absorbed.

5. Remove from heat, cover, and let stand 5 minutes. Before serving stir in lemon juice and cilantro.

Serves 4 to 6. Serve with raita.

**(Per serving) Calories: 285; Protein: 8g; Fat: 5g;
Carbohydrates: 51g; Cholesterol: 0mg; Sodium: 349mg.**

RAITA

CUCUMBER AND YOGURT SALAD

Prep Time: 10 minutes
Cook Time: None

3 cups plain nonfat yogurt,
   drained well with cheesecloth
   or a strainer
1 cucumber, peeled, seeded,
   and grated

½ cup minced fresh mint leaves
1 hot green chili, seeded and
   minced, if desired
Salt to taste

In a bowl combine all the ingredients. Serve with Couscous Upma.

Makes about 4 cups.

**(Per serving) Calories: 78; Protein: 7g; Fat: 1g;
Carbohydrates: 10g; Cholesterol: 2mg; Sodium: 135mg.**

JIMMY'S HABIBI KABOBS

These kabobs are a cross between Middle Eastern ones and spicy appetizers served at Italian restaurants like the Bricciola in Milan. They are great for making sandwiches or eating over steamed spinach.

Prep Time: 15 minutes
Cook Time: 22 minutes

2 pounds ground veal

¼ cup minced fresh parsley

3 tablespoons bread crumbs

2 large eggs, beaten lightly

2 teaspoons finely minced garlic

2 teaspoons minced gingerroot

2 teaspoons ground coriander

1 tablespoon minced fresh oregano, or 1 teaspoon dried oregano, crumbled

½ teaspoon Herbes de Provence

½ teaspoon lemon pepper seasoning

Juice of 1 lemon, or to taste

Salt to taste

Assorted vegetables, such as green or red bell pepper, cherry tomatoes, zucchini, and onion, all cubed except tomatoes, for the kabobs, as desired

Vegetable oil to taste

1. Preheat the oven to 400°F.

2. In a bowl combine the veal, parsley, bread crumbs, eggs, garlic, ginger-root, coriander, oregano, Herbes de Provence, lemon pepper, lemon juice, and salt. With dampened hands, form the mixture into meatballs, each about 2 inches in diameter.

3. Arrange four meatballs interspersed with vegetables of choice, except tomatoes, on six long skewers and place in a baking pan. Brush kabobs with vegetable oil.

4. Bake the kabobs for 20 minutes, or until juices run clear. If desired, add cherry tomatoes and place under a preheated broiler about 3 to 4 inches from the heat for 2 to 3 minutes, turning, until golden brown.

Serves 6.

(Per serving) Calories: 267; Protein: 32g; Fat: 12g; Carbohydrates: 5g; Cholesterol: 185mg; Sodium: 256mg.

PAPA AL COUSCOUS

Prep Time: *10 minutes*
Cook Time: *35 to 40 minutes*

2 tablespoons olive oil

5 whole garlic cloves, smashed

2 (about ¾ pound) zucchini, cubed

4 medium-large tomatoes, or 8 large
   (about 2 pounds) plum tomatoes,
   cut into 1-inch pieces

1 tablespoon minced fresh oregano,
   or 1 teaspoon dried oregano,
   crumbled

1 teaspoon lemon pepper

½ teaspoon Herbes de Provence

Salt and pepper to taste

4½ to 5 cups water

3 Knorr chicken bouillon cubes

2 bay leaves

1 cup couscous

Juice of ½ lemon, or to taste

⅓ cup minced fresh parsley leaves

Extra-virgin olive oil for drizzling

MOROCCO

◆

96

In a casserole set over moderate heat, warm the oil until it is hot. Add the garlic cloves and cook, stirring, until golden. Add the zucchini and cook, stirring occasionally, for 3 minutes, or until softened. Add the tomatoes, oregano, lemon pepper, Herbes de Provence, and salt and pepper to taste, and cook the mixture, stirring occasionally, for 5 minutes more. Add the water, bouillon cubes, bay leaves, and additional salt and pepper to taste, if desired, and simmer the mixture, stirring occasionally, for 15 minutes. Add the couscous and continue cooking, stirring occasionally, until it reaches porridgelike consistency—about 5 to 10 minutes. Add the lemon juice and parsley. Discard the bay leaves. Serve the couscous drizzled with the extra-virgin olive oil and dusted with freshly grated pepper.

Serves 4.

(Per serving) Calories: 332; Protein: 10g; Fat: 8g;
Carbohydrates: 57g; Cholesterol: 0mg; Sodium: 1006mg.

WILD MUSHROOM COUSCOUS

Prep Time: *10 minutes*
Cook Time: *20 to 25 minutes*

2 tablespoons olive oil

1 onion, minced

³/₄ pound Portobello or white
   mushrooms, trimmed, wiped clean
   and sliced

Salt and freshly ground black
   pepper to taste

1 Italian sweet turkey sausage,
   sliced

5 cups water

2 Knorr chicken bouillon cubes

1 teaspoon Herbes de Provence

¹/₄ teaspoon red pepper flakes,
   or to taste

¹/₂ teaspoon lemon pepper

1²/₃ cups couscous

3 tablespoons snipped fresh dill

Extra-virgin olive oil for drizzling
   as garnish

Freshly grated Parmesan to taste,
   as garnish

In a large nonstick skillet set over moderate heat, warm the oil until hot. Add the onion and cook, stirring, 5 minutes. Add the mushrooms and salt and pepper to taste and cook, stirring occasionally, for 5 minutes more. Add the sausage and cook, stirring, until no longer pink. Add the water, bouillon cubes, Herbes de Provence, red pepper flakes, and lemon pepper, bring to a boil and simmer, stirring for 2 minutes. Add the couscous and simmer, stirring occasionally until tender. Before serving stir in the dill. Serve the couscous in bowls, drizzled with extra-virgin olive oil and freshly grated Parmesan if desired.

Serves 4 to 6.

(Per serving) **Calories: 275; Protein: 10g; Fat: 6g;
Carbohydrates: 44g; Cholesterol: 7mg; Sodium: 507mg.**

After a perfect meal we are more susceptible to the ecstasy of love than at any other time.

—Dr. Hans Bazli

I'm not a big sweet eater. I usually skip dessert, and I suppose in that sense I'm lucky to save on the calories. I have friends with enormous sweet tooths; Daniele rarely skips dessert, often selecting restaurants based on their dessert menus. I patiently watch as he devours his favourite mousse or cake, not seeing what all the fuss is about. So since I have little experience in creating desserts, I have begged and borrowed recipes and combed my kitchen for a few as well. Unfortunately, these are not all low fat and perhaps a bit sinful to the waistline, but as always I advocate moderation rather than extremism at the table. I'd rather have two bites of something good than a plate full of cardboard.

WARM INDIAN RICE PUDDING

Prep Time: 5 minutes
Cook Time: 30 minutes

1 cup short-grain Indian or
  Italian (Arborio) rice*

1½ cups water

2 to 3 cups milk

½ cup sugar, or to taste

¼ cup golden raisins

¼ cup raw cashews or shelled
  pistachios, chopped fine

Seeds from 4 cardamom pods

Ground cinnamon to taste

In a saucepan combine the rice and water, bring to a boil, stirring, and simmer, stirring occasionally, for 15 minutes. Add 2 cups of the milk, the sugar, raisins, cashews or pistachios, cardamom seeds, and cinnamon, and simmer, stirring often, for 10 to 15 minutes more, or until rice is tender and mixture creamy. Add additional milk, if necessary. Pudding may also be served chilled.

Serves 4 to 6.

*Arborio or Indian short-grain rice is available at specialty food shops.

**(Per serving) Calories: 276; Protein: 6g; Fat: 5g;
Carbohydrates: 51g; Cholesterol: 11mg; Sodium: 43mg.**

PINEAPPLE SORBET

Prep Time: *10 minutes*
Cook Time: *None*

1 pineapple (about 3½ pounds)

3 to 4 tablespoons sugar, or to taste

3 to 4 tablespoons fresh lemon juice,
   or to taste

1. Peel, core, and cube the pineapple.

2. In a food processor or blender, purée the pulp until smooth. Add the sugar and lemon juice to taste and process just to combine. Transfer mixture to ice cube trays and freeze until frozen.

3. Transfer frozen cubes to processor and process until light and fluffy. Pack in a freezer container and freeze until ready to serve.

Makes about 1 quart.

(Per serving) Calories: 70; Protein: 1g; Fat: 1g;
Carbohydrates: 18g; Cholesterol: 0mg; Sodium: 1mg.

ORANGE
SORBET

Prep Time: 10 to 12 minutes
Cook Time: 5 to 7 minutes

2 ounces sugar cubes
   (about thirty ½-inch cubes)
6 navel oranges
3 to 4 tablespoons fresh lemon juice

1. Rub the sugar cubes over the surface of 5 of the oranges until each cube is orange colored. Grate the rind from the remaining orange. Squeeze enough of the oranges to yield 2 cups juice.

2. In a saucepan set over moderate heat, combine 1 cup of the juice with the sugar cubes and cook, stirring, until sugar is completely dissolved. Transfer mixture to a bowl, stir in remaining juice and grated rind, and chill until cold.

3. Transfer mixture to an ice cream freezer and freeze according to manufacturer's instructions. Or freeze in ice cube trays as in Pineapple Sorbet.

Makes about 2 cups.

(Per serving) Calories: 164; Protein: 2g; Fat: 1g;
Carbohydrates: 42g; Cholesterol: 0mg; Sodium: 3mg.

STRAWBERRY SORBET

Prep Time: *8 to 10 minutes*
Cook Time: *5 minutes*

1 cup sugar, or to taste
1 cup water
1½ pints strawberries, hulled and sliced
3 to 4 tablespoons fresh lemon juice,
   or to taste

1. In a saucepan set over moderate heat, combine the sugar and water, bring mixture to a boil, and simmer, stirring, for 3 minutes, or until clear. Transfer to a bowl and let cool.

2. In a food processor or blender purée the strawberries with lemon juice to taste. Add strawberry purée to sugar syrup and stir to combine.

3. Transfer mixture to an ice cream freezer and freeze according to package directions. Or freeze in ice cube trays as in Pineapple Sorbet.

Makes about 1 quart.

(Per serving) Calories: 152; Protein: 1g; Fat: 1g;
Carbohydrates: 38g; Cholesterol: 0mg; Sodium: 3mg.

MANGO
PARFAIT

Prep Time: *15 minutes*
Cook Time: *None*

3 cups diced mango (about 2 pounds
  mangoes, peeled and cubed)

2 tablespoons fresh lime juice

1 to 2 tablespoons honey,
  or to taste

⅛ to ¼ teaspoon ground cinnamon,
  or to taste

2 cups vanilla yogurt

Fresh mint leaves for garnish
  (optional)

1. In a food processor or blender purée the mango until smooth and transfer it to a bowl. Add the lime juice, honey, and cinnamon to the mango purée and stir to combine. Chill until ready to assemble parfaits.

2. **To assemble parfaits:** In parfait or stemmed glasses spoon a 1-inch-thick layer of yogurt, top with a layer of mango and repeat layering. Chill until ready to serve. Garnish with fresh mint leaves, if desired.

Serves 4.

(Per serving) Calories: 137; Protein: 7g; Fat: 1g;
Carbohydrates: 28g; Cholesterol: 2mg; Sodium: 89mg.

CHAMBORD BERRIES IN CREAM

Prep Time: *5 to 8 minutes*

Cook Time: *7 to 8 minutes*

1 pint strawberries,
  hulled and sliced

1/2 pint raspberries,
  rinsed and picked over

1/2 pint blueberries,
  rinsed and picked over

1/3 to 1/2 cup sugar,
  or to taste

1/2 cup Chambord liqueur

8 scoops frozen vanilla yogurt
  or ice cream

1. In a saucepan combine the strawberries, raspberries, blueberries, and sugar, bring mixture to a simmer over moderately low heat, stirring gently, and simmer until sugar begins to dissolve. Add the liqueur and simmer, stirring occasionally, for 3 minutes.

2. Arrange ice cream in 4 serving dishes and immediately spoon hot sauce over it.

Serves 4.

(Per serving) Calories: 338; Protein: 12g; Fat: 1g;
Carbohydrates: 70g; Cholesterol: 4mg; Sodium: 159mg.

RASPBERRY TART

Prep Time: 15 minutes,
             plus 30 minutes chilling time
Cook Time: 25 minutes

For the pastry:

1¼ cups all-purpose flour

¼ teaspoon salt

1 stick (½ cup) unsalted butter,
    cut into bits

4 tablespoons ice water

2 pints raspberries

⅔ cup red currant jelly

2 tablespoons Eau de Vie des
    Framboises, or Chambord liqueur
    (optional)

Frozen yogurt or ice cream as an
    accompaniment (optional)

1. **Make the pastry:** Into a bowl sift the flour and salt. Add the butter and with a pastry blender or your fingertips, blend the mixture until it resembles coarse meal. Add the water and stir until mixture forms a ball. On a lightly floured surface gently knead dough until it is smooth. Chill, wrapped in plastic, for 30 minutes.

2. Preheat oven to 400°F.

3. On a lightly floured surface roll out dough into a round ⅛-inch thick and fit it into a 9-inch tart pan with a removable bottom. Prick the pastry and line it with wax paper. Weight the paper with raw rice or dried beans and bake the shell for 15 minutes. Remove paper and rice and continue to bake for 10 to 15 minutes more, or until golden. Transfer to a rack to cool.

4. Arrange the berries in the tart shell. In a small saucepan set over moderate heat, combine the jelly and the Eau de Vie or Chambord, if desired, and simmer the mixture, stirring, until smooth and thick. Drizzle the glaze over the berries and serve the tart with frozen yogurt or ice cream, if desired.

Serves 8.

(Per serving) Calories: 272; Protein: 3g; Fat: 12g;
Carbohydrates: 38g; Cholesterol: 33mg; Sodium: 80mg.

RASPBERRY
SAUCE

Prep Time: *5 minutes*
Cook Time: *None*

Two 10-ounce packages frozen raspberries,
    thawed and drained
2 tablespoons fresh lemon juice,
    or to taste
2 to 3 tablespoons superfine sugar,
    or to taste
1 to 2 tablespoons Eau de Vie des Framboises
    (optional)

In a food processor or blender, purée the raspberries. Strain the sauce
through a sieve into a bowl, pressing hard on the solids, and stir in the
lemon juice and sugar. Add Eau de Vie, if desired. Chill, covered, until
ready to serve.

Makes about 1 cup.

(Per serving) Calories: 86; Protein: 1g; Fat: 1g;
Carbohydrates: 22g; Cholesterol: 0mg; Sodium: 1mg.

POACHED PEARS WITH RASPBERRY SAUCE

Prep Time: *12 to 15 minutes*

Cook Time: *35 minutes*

For the poaching liquid:

2$^{1}/_{2}$ cups dry white wine

$^{1}/_{2}$ to $^{3}/_{4}$ cup sugar, or to taste
(depending upon ripeness
of pears)

1 vanilla bean, split lengthwise

1 cinnamon stick

1 tablespoon minced gingerroot

4 large firm-ripe pears
(Bosc or Bartlett), peeled and cored
from the blossom end but left whole

Raspberry Sauce
(see following page)

Toasted sliced almonds for garnish,
if desired

1. In a saucepan just large enough to hold the pears in one layer combine the wine, sugar, vanilla bean, cinnamon, and gingerroot, bring liquid to a boil, and simmer, stirring, until sugar is dissolved. Add pears, standing them in the liquid, and simmer, covered, for 30 minutes, or until just tender. Remove from heat and let cool in the pan.

2. Transfer pears to a bowl, strain poaching liquid over them and chill, covered, until ready to serve.

3. **To serve:** Arrange pears on serving plates, spoon Raspberry Sauce over them, and garnish with almonds.

Serves 4.

(Per serving) Calories: 451; Protein: 2g; Fat: 1g;
Carbohydrates: 91g; Cholesterol: 0mg; Sodium: 10mg.

APPLE GALLETTES

Prep Time: *15 minutes,*
                     plus 30 minutes chilling time

Cook Time: *30 to 35 minutes*

1 pound frozen puff pastry,
   thawed in the refrigerator

4 Golden Delicious apples, peeled,
   cored, and sliced very thin

¼ cup sugar, or to taste

3 tablespoons unsalted butter,
   cut into bits

For the glaze:

1 cup apricot preserves, strained

2 tablespoons dark rum or Cognac

3 tablespoons chopped pistachios
   (optional)

1. Halve the pastry and keep one half chilled while working with the remaining half. On a lightly floured surface gently roll the puff pastry ¼ inch thick, cut out two 7-inch rounds and transfer the rounds to a baking sheet. Repeat with remaining half of pastry. Chill for at least 30 minutes.

2. Preheat the oven to 400°F.

3. Arrange the apple slices decoratively on the pastry rounds in concentric circles, sprinkle each round with 1 tablespoon of the sugar and dot with some of the butter. Bake for 30 minutes, or until apples are golden brown and pastry cooked. Transfer to racks to cool.

4. In a saucepan set over moderate heat, combine the apricot preserves with the rum, and simmer the mixture, stirring, until smooth and thick. Gently brush the glaze over the tarts. Sprinkle the tarts with the pistachios before serving.

Serves 6 to 8.

(Per serving) **Calories: 322; Protein: 2.5g; Fat: 11g; Carbohydrates: 53g; Cholesterol: 25mg; Sodium: 64mg.**

Kalustyan's

When my mother moved to Manhattan in the early seventies, there was already an established Indian community in New York and an array of shops to serve its needs. But the only store I remember going to is Kalustyan's on Lexington Avenue. His tiny store had everything one could possibly want, and I remember longing to dig my hands into the bulk barrels of raisins every time we went there. They were always quite generous with children and handed out samples liberally.

When I moved back to New York from Europe, an added plus to my new apartment was that it was within walking distance from Kalustyan's. In fact, as soon as I moved in, I promptly walked down to Kalustyan's to fill my pantry with the basic spices and staples. The tiny store was just the same, with the big barrels of dried fruit and spicy pickles and chutneys lining the walls. And even though I was no longer a kid they were just as generous when it came to samples. I got in the habit of going there in the afternoon before lunch and often left too full to eat what I brought home. Going to Kalustyan's always cheered me when I was down, warmed me inside, and even now puts a smile on my face as I write this. When I went back to Europe it was the nice man at Kalustyan's that I called from Milan, desperate for the savories that I could find only there. He would mail me any spice or vacuum-packed food my heart desired. They always remembered me when I came in, and I always felt as if I were coming back home.

If I must pick only one store in the world where I could shop, it would be Kalustyan's. He is my favorite. I have gone to many pretentious gourmet shops and specialty food stores in many places but I find the humble excellence of that shop quite rare. And I am pleased to write that one need not live in the city to benefit from his large collection of goods. One can now order anything to be sent anywhere in the world. They are quite good about doing their best and finding whatever ingredient their customers ask for. I include here their phone number and fax so that all the ingredients to any of the recipes contained in this book can be easily found. And say hello from me.

Kalustyan's
123 Lexington Avenue (at 28th Street)   Telephone: (212) 685-3451
New York, NY 10016   Fax: (212) 683-8458

Index